Copyright © 2022 Todd Kachinski Kottmeier

All rights reserved. No part of this publication may be reproduced or transmitted in any form or by any means, electronic or mechanical, including photocopy, recording, or any information storage and retrieval system, without permission in writing from the publisher.

First Edition.

ISBN: 9798843739225

DRAG411 asked each of the performers in this book to reach out to the entertainers around them to involve them in this book that will be printed annually. We offered to publish for free any person that sent one in. We are constantly creating new books and need the input of entertainers. All they have to do is go to the DRAG411 group on facebook (not the DRAG411 page) to simply participate.

CONTENT CO-CREATED BY: Addy Pose, Aja Jem Pizzazz, Allure Gic, Andrew Martinez, Andronica Glitoris, Angel Sexton, Anna Flactic-Shoqqqq, Annie Christ, Atlas Midos, Averi AyCock, Ben Poison'd, Bryce Culver, Cameron Ticey, Candi Lachey, Carter Bachmann, Chaella Montgomery-Kohl, Chasen Lewis, Clint Torris, Coco B. Della Notte, Dante Inferno, Dawsin A. Diamud, Demonica de Baum, Desiree Mathews, Diego Wolf, Donny Mirassou, Fancy Kakes, Fluxx Wyldly, Grandma Pearl, Hayden Lee Sunshine, Howie Felon-Luv, Humble Izreal, Irish Lashez, Ivy Dripp, Jackie Divine Diamond, James Cass, Jason Beauregard, Jazzmine Lavender, Jessica Emms, Jushtin Butterfly, Justice Twist, Justin Case, Justin Tyme, Justyn Ashtyn, Kade Jackwell, Kai, Kelly Powers, Kilda Mann, Killa Watt, King Vaughnz Spanic, Kitty DeVil, Kitty Quinn Khrystian, KJ Mac, Krystal Cain, Leiyana Santana, Levi U. Wantan Moore, Lili Whyte, Logan Rider, Lord Severus, Maya M. Monroe, Mike Hawk, Mira Shatters, Mischa Michaels, Miss Domeaner, Mistress Detta, Miya Motions, Mona Del Rose, Mona Lotz, Mondo Millions, Monèt Love, Morgan Davis, Morganna Pheeling Tarclure, Mr. Killing Ya Softly, Mrs. PurrZsa Kyttyn Azrael, Mya Chanel Lamour, Nik El, Nikolette Kilz, Nipples La Rue, Noah Fear, Oliver Steerpike, Olivia Logan, Ouija Ornias Michaels, Parris B. Cbello, Patricia Del Rosario, Pierce Gabriel, Prinze Valentino, Rebel Love Diva, Rebel Rose, Rockell Blu, Rosemary Galore, Sassy Black, Sean Wolff, Seymour Chilton, Seymour Rainbows, Shire Paige,, Sister Angela Merici, Sondra St. James, Special K Culver, STACI, Tara Byte, Tasha Dane, Teri Taylor, Tobe Danieles, Tonna McKenzie, Travis Hard, Veronica Foxxx, Vicki Vincent, Warumono, Wendy G Kennedy, Whiskey Richards, Xyvien, and Zizi Foxx.

DRAG411.com
InfamousTodd.com

Letter from DRAG411

I don't charge performers to be involved in these books. I go online and beg for a month to become involved with each book. Once a person commits, I plead with them to ask their mentors and peers to become involved.

When I created my 10th DRAG book, DRAG Bully, which was my 30th book I thought I was done. The doctors had diagnosed me with onset dementia and I was struggling. I believed it was a good time to wrap up the DRAG411 project and give it a rest. Medication and therapy have granted me a window into giving me confidence to create new projects. I do not know which project will be my last, but I say… "let's race this car until the wheels fall off."

New books will become reality, if you have the patience to deal with me. This year we already created "The DRAG Book," "DRAG SHOW," the 2022 "Who's Who of DRAG" directory, this book, and the group is working on a book called, "DRAG 2.0" The Future of Drag and the upcoming 2023 "Who's Who of DRAG." It is hard for me to stay focused so I have the performers make it easy on me. There is no way I can individually contact thousands of them. I don't have those files anymore since coming out of retirement. I have to rely on them participating in the DRAG411 group (not the page) on Facebook. Feel free to join it as a performer or a fan. In the group they can post all their responses in one place for me to access for each book.

It never cost any money to be involved with DRAG411. I make my money when a book sells. I thank you for buying this book. The "Who's Who of DRAG" series will be my new platform. The performers in the International "Who's Who of DRAG" Directory were asked to provide information to help the readers. They decided what information they would share with you. I personally asked them to provide their official stage name, the part of the world they are from since DRAG411 is over 7,000 performers in 32 countries, how to follow them on social media, titles they won, something personal about themselves, ways to contact them for books, a close up/head shot (with a photo credit, if someone talented took the picture of them), their goals, motivations… and so much more.

I hope you find these 111 performers both sincere and insightful. Pretend you are sitting in a room as the discuss their insight. To follow their story, make the time to go online and find them. Do me a favor, let them know you noticed them in this book. Let them know they made a difference. I promise you, everybody in this book wants to make a difference in your life. Thank you for making a difference in my life as a reader.

Infamous Todd Kachinski Kottmeier
Founder of DRAG411
DRAG411.com

I dedicate this 13th book* to the following 111 DRAG performers that contributed to this book by sharing their story, their truth.

Addy Pose, Aja Jem Pizzazz, Allure Gic, Andrew Martinez, Andronica Glitoris, Angel Sexton, Anna Flactic-Shoqqqq, Annie Christ, Atlas Midos, Averi AyCock, Ben Poison'd, Bryce Culver, Cameron Ticey, Candi Lachey, Carter Bachmann, Chaella Montgomery-Kohl, Chasen Lewis, Clint Torris, Coco B. Della Notte, Dante Inferno, Dawsin A. Diamud, Demonica de Baum, Desiree Mathews, Diego Wolf, Donny Mirassou, Fancy Kakes, Fluxx Wyldly, Grandma Pearl, Hayden Lee Sunshine, Howie Felon-Luv, Humble Izreal, Irish Lashez, Ivy Dripp, Jackie Divine Diamond, James Cass, Jason Beauregard, Jazzmine Lavender, Jessica Emms, Jushtin Butterfly, Justice Twist, Justin Case, Justin Tyme, Justyn Ashtyn, Kade Jackwell, Kai, Kelly Powers, Kilda Mann, Killa Watt, King Vaughnz Spanic, Kitty DeVil, Kitty Quinn Khrystian, KJ Mac, Krystal Cain, Leiyana Santana, Levi U. Wantan Moore, Lili Whyte, Logan Rider, Lord Severus, Maya M. Monroe, Mike Hawk, Mira Shatters, Mischa Michaels, Miss Domeaner, Mistress Detta, Miya Motions, Mona Del Rose, Mona Lotz, Mondo Millions, Monèt Love, Morgan Davis, Morganna Pheeling Tarclure, Mr. Killing Ya Softly, Mrs. PurrZsa Kyttyn Azrael, Mya Chanel Lamour, Nik El, Nikolette Kilz, Nipples La Rue, Noah Fear, Oliver Steerpike, Olivia Logan, Ouija Ornias Michaels, Parris B. Cbello, Patricia Del Rosario, Pierce Gabriel, Prinze Valentino, Rebel Love Diva, Rebel Rose, Rockell Blu, Rosemary Galore, Sassy Black, Sean Wolff, Seymour Chilton, Seymour Rainbows, Shire Paige,, Sister Angela Merici, Sondra St. James, Special K Culver, STACI, Tara Byte, Tasha Dane, Teri Taylor, Tobe Danieles, Tonna McKenzie, Travis Hard, Veronica Foxxx, Vicki Vincent, Warumono, Wendy G Kennedy, Whiskey Richards, Xyvien, and Zizi Foxx.

*13th book. Does not include the Who's Who of DRAG Directory series.

The Ten Chapters

One: "How bad does your depression get at its worse." *Page 3*

Two: "When do you realize that your depression is not just feeling down for a moment?" *p. 21*

Three: "Did you think DRAG would help you with your depression before you began doing DRAG?" *p. 31*

Four: "How do you handle preparing to do DRAG when you feel depressed?" *p. 41*

Five: "What does DRAG do for you to deal with your depression when you are not on stage?" *p. 51*

Six: "How does dressing up help you to deal with depression?" *p.60*

Seven: "How does performing help you deal with depression?" *p.70*

Eight: "How does social media, as your DRAG persona, help you deal with depression?" *p. 78*

Nine: "People will assume that DRAG is a cure-all from depression. Can you explain if sometimes it does not work?" *p. 86*

Ten: "How do the fans help you with your depression?" *p. 94*

Chapter One, Question One
"How bad does your depression get at its worse."

❀Had a plastic bag taped around my head. Twisted my hands in a rope behind my back knowing it would take too long to unwrangle it before the oxygen left the grocery store sack. Terrible way to die. A fire in your chest. Someone that was not supposed to be in my home arrived and something told him to break in. He found my body. That was one of several trips to therapy. I kept trying to kill myself. It was not until they put me on medications would I find my way out of the rabbit hole.

❀ My depression has been very severe since I was eleven years old. In my teens, my depression sparked a psychotic episode which has continued to be a trend to this day. When my depression sparks a psychotic episode, I'm not only feeling my absolute worst but I struggle to access support because I lose the ability to recognize who and what is real or who and what is another hallucination or delusion. It really feels like I've gone through every stereotypical depressed behavior. I've abused alcohol and painkillers, I've attempted and harmed myself, and I've destroyed relationships to push people away. I've also found sanctuary in my art, like so many depressed artists and performers before me.

❀ I have suffered from depression for years. I am currently taking medication to help control it. The problem with the meds is the depression is still there, it's just you're too high to care. I'm not real fond of them. I go on and off them quite a bit. My lowest point was when my partner passed away of cancer. I tried to kill myself but was lucky and a friend found me. Normally when my depression hits, I lock myself in my bedroom, and stay there in bed. It generally lasts two to three days.

❀ At my lowest, I have thought what it would be like to just vanish. I have sat in my room, I lay down, I close my eyes, put my fingers in my ears so I can't hear anything and just pretend that I have never been born. That I have never been a burden. I have a really big family and I have taken care of everyone else yet never taken care of me. At my worst, I thought what would be the easiest way to die. The first time I attempted suicide I was nine years old. I skipped school and close to the school was a train track. I sat in the middle of it and waited for a train. No train. I went home and the abuse of my father just continued. The second time I was fourteen. In my young mind I thought a whole bottle of Tylenol would do it. Threw up for hours.

The third time was my first open stage with Judges. I had worked for so many years to get to where I am. It took me two weeks of non-stop work on my costumes. I picked the perfect songs. It seemed like everything was going just right! Well needless to say I did not win. What destroyed me was the original scores wrote down had been scribbled out and new lower scores added. I felt betrayed, and humiliated. I went home and made sure everyone was asleep. I grabbed a kitchen knife and went into the bathroom. I sat on the floor crying like I was five years old again. My son knocked on the bathroom door and simply said I love you! Those were my lowest points. At that moment I realized that I would only hurt the ones I love and it was not worth hurting them. I have suffered from depression all my life but have been told I have post-traumatic stress disorder (PTSD) from the insurmountable abuse I suffered my whole young life. I don't take anything because I don't want pills to decide my life for me. I use love and friendship to get me through.

❀ My depression can get so bad that I skip shows, silence messenger, and start thinking of which freeway bridge is the closest to me.

❀ At its worst, I don't leave my room for days and live off whatever chips I have in my home. I'm usually active on social media, but at its worst I'll just stare at the wall for what feels like hours. I don't talk to my friends either, and it takes a while to fully shake myself out of that kind of funk.

❀ At my worst I turned to a full month's prescription of Xanax and a handle of Rich and Rare Whiskey. I was sure I was doing everyone a favor because I was certain my presence was an annoyance; at best, they would probably celebrate my departure. So, I ate the pills and chugged the booze and started a nice warm tub. If nothing else worked, I would drown when I passed out. I wanted to be sure there was no way I could mess it up like I had messed up everything else. I am so glad I didn't know my nosy neighbor had kept a copy of my key and was concerned when I didn't answer their call. They let themselves in, dragged me from the tub, made me vomit and called 911. It was one of the first times I believed someone could love me without needing anything from me.

❀ At its worst, it makes me feel like I'm only alive as a means of production. I feel like performer friends only like me because I'm physically present (and performing for their show), even though deep down I know it isn't true. It often happens, to be honest.

❦ At its worst, I cannot get out of bed. I won't want to do anything and will trap myself in my own thoughts. I was diagnosed at twenty with Moderate to Severe depression and there are days where it hits me super hard. Sometimes I feel that if I could disappear, nobody would care.

❦ At its worst my depression has put me in the hospital. I have had four unaliving events since the age of sixteen. The last being about three years ago. I downed medication and ended up hospitalized for two days to get the medication out of my system then a few days in the psych ward.

❦ I will shut everyone out in a downward spiral and I don't even realize it until I'm already there. I become a hermit, very reclusive and will go off the radar for months.

❦ Depression combined with ADHD is the absolute worst. A common side dish for ADHD is RSD (Rejection Sensitivity Disphoria). Often, my mind will decide that nobody likes/loves me, nobody wants to see me, nobody wants to be my friend, and that I have nothing to offer the world. As I have gotten older, I have a tendency to think my ship has sailed, and my ability to achieve anything else is on board. Isolation is always easy for me and allows negative thoughts a place to flourish. Projects pile up and become overwhelming. Sometimes, it's all I can do to accomplish one thing per day. Life is a struggle, but it ebbs and flows. I have to try harder than seemingly everyone to do the simplest things. I'm constantly reminding myself things will get better despite not being very optimistic they actually will. I'm not an alcoholic, but I read the AA Big Book. It was kind of a manual for life. I practice many of those principles to manage my depression and cope.

❦ My depression gets horrible. I am a multiple suicide attempt survivor. I began being a cutter when I was around the age of eight. I never understood why I was so depressed. I knew I was different and I knew I didn't belong. Back then we didn't talk about things. I had my first real suicide attempt around seventeen. When I was twenty, I found drag and realized the term, "transgender." Came out as trans and hit the stage and never looked backed. I had my last suicide attempt in 2013 before I started hormones. I have not tried since I started hormones and went back to performing after a five-year break from the stage.

❦ At my worst, I literally can't function as a person. It could last hours or weeks. It comes in waves. I never know when it's going to hit and usually ends up in me self-harming.

❀ My depression can be a heartbreaking 48 hour long where I get scared and not leave the house for weeks.

❀ My depression hits a very big high. There was a generation gap because of the AIDS crisis. Many people, including my peer died. Sometimes I feel very alone. The gay community and drag has changed. As I reach my fifties, it's very hard very hard to morph into this new generation. I try to be understanding, because I remember how it was when I was young. DRAG does help release that feeling because I do stage comedy. I can take much of the grief and depression and turn it into humor. I think you need to stand back sometimes and breathe. Through depression I learned to separate and understand that there is such a generation gap. It is only normal to feel the depression but not allow yourself to engulf yourself. I think my age group (and older) went through much more nonacceptance. Now that I am older, at times, I feel that it's hard to be accepted by the new generation.

❀At my worst years ago, I wanted to end it all. Over the years I've learned to cope better and current lows make me not want to do anything even if it's things I love. I don't want to read, create content, write, I just want to sit in a room and pretend the world doesn't exist. When I'm at that low, the amount of energy and spoons that goes into everyday life puts me into the negative some days. Spoons is like a physical manifestation of the mental energy it takes to do something. Like, getting out of bed for the day may take one spoon while a work meeting takes 2 or 3. Everyone has a different number of spoons and how many are required for activities

❀ At its worst, I cannot leave my bed for new opportunities. I can muddle through existing commitments, but I have no desire to expand or grow. I know that I would feel better if I applied to shows or made a new costume. It's just hard to want to keep going because when my depression is at its worst, I am too tired to see the point.

❀My depression hit at its worst when I was in my early to mid-twenties. I was really just starting to figure out who I was as a person, and starting to really explore creative outlets such as drag. I'd already tried the "quick highs" available, and nothing was working to make me snap out of it, not cocaine, GHB (gamma hydroxybutyrate), just to name a couple. I could not turn to my blood relatives because I was brought up in a super ultra conservative Church of God home. The other side of my family were super ultra conservative Southern Baptists; if I went to either I was doomed to be condemned to Hell or face possibly going to a conversion camp or something. I didn't know what they would do, or try to do. My roommate at that time was not too supportive and also was not in a good state of mind himself battling with his own depression and mental illnesses. I found myself instead of trying get better or pick myself up constantly depressing and repressing myself drinking to the point of blackening out not thinking until I woke up in a bathtub with a razor in my hand and marks up my right arm. During this time, I was a baby queen, and living in Birmingham, Alabama. I knew I had to get out of there. Losing my job, being evicted, my roommate having taken his own life; I seriously had nothing to lose. I went back up to Huntsville, Alabama where I'd first began drag, even before I was a baby queen. The first show I saw had three of my biggest and best mentors. One gave me a hug and told me welcome home, the others hugged me and told me how happy they were to see me and see I was back. Drag literally saved my life.

❀ I've attempted suicide many times. The most recent time I didn't actually stop myself. I just got sick and threw the drugs up I took. It took weeks to want to live again. I still doubt sometimes if it's worth it.

❀ I've been medicated for depression for several years now, so not nearly as bad as it was once. Suicidal thoughts used to be at least a weekly occurrence. The way I realized these weren't serious thoughts was "I've got a new dress I haven't worn...I can't go yet!" One day at a time, and there's always something to continue for no matter how small or shallow sounding.

❀ At its worst, I have trouble with motivation doing even the most basic tasks. Getting out of bed, taking a shower, even messaging my own friends back become a huge task. My closest friends, when they felt it was needed, physically forced me to get out of the house.

❀ I am a 45-year-old gay man. I came out roughly eight years ago. The day I came out was not planned. I had finally got to the point where I was done. I went to work, took any and all medications with me and no intention of going home after work. When my shift at work was nearly over, I gathered my thoughts and knew what was just ahead for me. I picked up my cellphone and for some reason I opened it up to a picture of my daughter. My guardian angel kicked me in the gut and I suddenly I became alive. I went home, told my wife at the time, gathered my belongings in 35 seconds. I was finally born. That night I called my daughter and her mom (mt first of three wives) and came out. Their response, "what took you so long?" Finally, being alive was liberating. Several years later I accepted that I was battling Bipolar. I am on medications; you know how it goes. The last eighteen months have had me in some very, very dark places in my mind. Chronically feeling like a failure, failing others, I had good friends turn on me, and being an Indigo child as well takes its toll. These last twelve weeks have brought me back to a person I love. I've made some great new friends and have been blessed by this new circle. No matter how low the tide goes, it always has to come back in. You are loved and wanted and all of us sharing our thoughts want you here too. Follow us, friend us, talk to us.

❀ My depression was pretty bad before I started preforming drag. It was so bad that I almost attempted suicide multiple times in middle school and high school. Once I was out of high-school the thoughts still circled my mind, especially after being raped right after my eighteenth birthday. I went through a self-destruct period right afterward. I spent several years trying to push my depression away. From the outside no one knew how bad it was, but on the inside, I was a ticking time bomb. It was hard to get out of bed, let alone take a shower or brush my teeth. I felt like I couldn't discuss my feelings with anyone, even my wife. After my first divorce I overdosed. I didn't believe there was anything left for me. The one person that vowed for better or worse left. She could handle how I was, let alone, me just coming out transgender. After this I went out seeking help. I spent a few years switching my medicine trying to find the right match until I finally had enough. I decided to go see a licensed physician to help me with my transition. She found that the depression was mostly from having gender dysphoria. Since fully transitioning and spending several years preforming drag my depression has decreased, but at times it comes creeping in. Not eating, troubles sleeping or over sleeping, not waiting to get out of bed or do anything I normally enjoy doing.

❀ When I first came out Drag was everything to me! Being that I'm in my 50's, the only label I had to identify with was being a gay male, but doing drag helped me express my true self through fashion, makeup and being an entertainer. Then as I turned 21, I learned that there were transgender women who were also entertaining. I blossomed from there. I was an exploding time bomb waiting to happen, so angry and depressed because I never fit in. However, I found my tribe of entertainers and friends who made me feel loved and taught me how to love myself and live one day at a time. Just remember "Even a Rock has a bad day!"

❀ My depression actually started and was at its worst when I was still in school. During fourth grade, I started to become depressed and I didn't like myself at all but I was prescribed medication which greatly helped me out. I entered high school and was severely bullied for being different and that made me extremely depressed and suicidal. The school knew how bad the bullying was becoming but they chose to not help me and decided to blame me for it. That made me feel worthless and I had thoughts about ending it all by killing myself since I had no one to talk to. Every time I tried to say anything, all I'd hear was, "Shut up! No one cares." I eventually just stopped talking to other kids and I was using all my energy just to literally survive the day. There was even one day where I had decided to just kill myself in the middle of the room. I was taking a cooking class and we were using knives on that day. I took a chef's knife and just stood in the middle of the room holding the knife and staring at it and my wrist for at least twenty minutes. I ended up not being able to do it but that isn't the thing that still haunts me to this day. The part that still bothers me and hurts the most is that literally no one noticed me holding a knife and staring at it for half the period. No one cared enough to see if I was okay. It took ten years after graduating high school and years of therapy before I could actually love who I am and know that people do like me. They can see the creative and expressive side of me that all the bullies forced me to hide.

❀ Being autistic, emotions are extremely hard. When I chemically don't make the right ratio (on my own without medication) I don't even come close to feeling of happy. My lows can get dark like three of my six stays in the nut hut which were related to suicide attempts or thoughts. The fun part is my body metabolizes antidepressants in 24 hours so they don't help at all.

❀ I always live in some level of depression. From starting my adolescence knowing I was different at a very young age, trying to deal with my sexuality on my own, being beaten up for trying to live my truth, the deaths of my mother, father, brother, and sister, it seems I can't shack depression. I can get really low but I am very good at hiding it. Depression has become a part of me and at my lowest, I over do everything, eating, drinking, smoking, but worse of all, I want to hide. I want to be left alone. I can't face the world.

❀ At worst my depression has me where I just want to lay down and cry. I end up putting myself down because my depression forces me to think that I'm not good enough and when someone tries to comfort me, I take all my anger and frustration out on them. I've had my depression telling me I'm not good enough and that I can't do anything right. It gets me to the point where I start to shut down mentally and all I want to do is sleep and binge eat.

Depression has gotten so bad at some points I just want to die. It makes me feel like no one would care if I did or not die.

❀ I have battled with depression, Complex posttraumatic stress disorder (C-PTSD) and the extreme mental health symptoms of premenstrual dysphoric disorder since I was a child. At its worst, I collapse inward into the deepest despair and feeling of mourning, pain and exhaustion and I want to give up. I've tried to die. I have been hospitalized for my safety. I imagined no possible future for myself, I robbed myself of all hope.

❀ When I start to feel the depression setting in, I start to think negative and be really hard on myself to the point I have to tell myself not to think negatively because I am better than that. Being openly trans my depression hits pretty hard because my body doesn't match my gender and it's a constant depression struggle and battle.

❀ I feel that my anxiety and depression is due to issues in ROGER PIATTs life (my given name). Being Vivki Vincent really helps ease things. I'm forever grateful for my chosen family of sisters that are my therapy. I've invested forty years of my life into doing DRAG and my blessings abound. Retirement from being an entertainer was like a hard punch to the stomach. My PTSD stems from the horror of my childhood. Drag was always my escape from reality. You must try to put your personal hurt in life on a back burner somewhere. Drag became my crutches to my own survival. The applause from the crowd drowned out my sorrow. I've been a perfectionist at all my endeavors. I needed DRAG to help me escape. I dove deep into pageantry to hopefully, shine bright enough, to be impressive. I never aspired to be a woman, I'm an actor. Folks never really know the pain you're suffering hiding behind a face full of makeup. I'm estranged from my own family because I pushed their buttons. My poor mother went through hell because I was born gay, started doing female impersonation, was attracted to men of color and wanted to become famous. When the make-up and hair come off, I'm still a farm raised country boy. I sought validation through drag. Just know, there is no such thing as perfection, no matter how hard you try. Nobody wants their feelings walked on. The abyss of depression is always there. You either crawl out of that ditch and shine or you let it consume you. The price you pay to be popular isn't always pretty. The audience and the applause helped me be the masked singer. I had to put on my big girl panties, pull up my boot straps and get over myself. Depression is a demon that must be fought every day. Let yourself be inspired by those around you. It's sink or swim. I choose to swim with everything I've got. Professional help is always recommended, take the "happy" pills too. The demon of depression is a monster but it can be beaten and defeated. I'm a very blessed fella to have attained everything, every pageant and every crown I've competed to win. As I grow older, that demon still tries to get me. Don't let it!

❀ I withdraw from everything. I put up walls. I think if I make myself invisible no one will see my problems because they are too inconvenient to deal with for someone else. This is a combination of anxiety and PTSD. I'm not used to seeking help and know I need it. I am afraid to open up because it hurt me in the past. Sometimes I cope with bad Band-Aids like drinking or total isolation. I know I can't do that because it only hurts myself longer.

❀ At its worst, my depression literally confines me to a bed. I don't move, I don't get out from under the blankets. I have to call someone to take care of the dog. They try to help me make a start in getting out of the depression so that I can attempt to function around the house, even though I won't leave the house. Though, calling someone to help in this manner always makes me feel guilty and worse initially, but my friends are great with making me feel better about it. I end up buying them food or something as a thank you.

❀ When fighting my depression my brain is so negative. It tells me that my attempts at life, work and drag are useless and I'm all alone. I want to be comfortable around my drag family, without my brain saying, they don't really like you, they just tolerate you. They don't want to talk to you. You have no worth to them. You'll just disappoint them. My brain tells me I am not worth anything. That I'm not good enough. I wonder all the time, what they think of me. Are they talking about me behind my back? It feels like I've lost my soul somewhere. And my heart is broken. I am broken.

❀ I deal with a lot of gender dysphoria and childhood trauma. Because of this I can fall into a frozen state of despair. At my worst, I have made up outlandish stories to get out of going to events, work, school, anything. I don't really have any answers but I've recently signed up at a counseling center to see about getting help. It's important to know you're not alone. It's ok to accept help. No journey is the same. You are loved.

❀ Sometimes my depression gets really bad that I shut down and shut everyone out and I do a total reset. If it's too much to handle I have reached out to friends for help.

❀ When I get too depressed, I go into a downward spiral. It's like I'm on a roller coaster of thoughts and emotions that never stop. I want to lock myself up in my bedroom, not eat and listen to metal music. Medicine is not my cure, but music and performing is my medicine.

❀ I literally do not want to get out of bed. I don't want to see anyone, I don't want to work, all I want to do is sleep.

❀ At my worst, my depression gets really bad. I don't even want to do anything for myself. Shower. Eat. Go anywhere. Cook. Nothing. Sometimes it gets so bad that myself destructive behaviors come back. I'm self-loathing. More than normal. Everything feels like it's my fault.

❀ Wanting to turn my phone off for the day. I lay in bed all day and just cry. I've hit this point where I accept all things as my fault. I've gotten to the place where I just screamed so loud that I made myself cry and lost my voice.

❀ Depression is complex, and can have many factors. The worst of it being a feeling of total helplessness, sadness, or self-hatred. It can feel like literally drowning with everyone watching and no one to help. It is very difficult to overcome at times. It can cause physical symptoms and other health complications as well, especially with chronic depression or other depression disorders.

❀ My depression causes my "inner voices" to turn on me. At my worst, I feel like an inconvenience, my existence is a mistake, and that everyone secretly hates me. I also get in the mindset that I am nothing but a provider to others and as soon as I stop being useful, then I become a disposable burden. I contemplate suicide with vivid details such as how I would prepare my assets, finances and personal belongings prior to my death and also the manner in which I would end my life.

❀ I have been on medication for ten years at this point. I don't tend to get really bad any more, but it does definitely impede my life even with medication. I find myself bored, lonely, frustrated, and hopeless with little to no provocation for it. I do get out of bed and put clothes on every day, but sometimes that is literally all I do. In the rare occasions I am without my medication, I cry for hours because it feels like the entire world is just waiting for me to fail.

❀Depression can hit out of nowhere. I've had moments where I feel that everyone is out having fun without me and I tend to follow made up scenarios in my head. Leading me to acting impulsively and at times, losing friendships.

❦ At my worst I've been suicidal and had very distorted thoughts. Where my mind made me responsible for everything that ever happened to me. I am overcome with thoughts that everyone hates me and everyone would be better off without me. It robs you of anything good. I have attempted suicide five times. One particular time I was rushed to the emergency room in critical condition. Those were some of the darkest days of my life. When everything gets so bad all I want is for everything to stop. In those moments death seems the only way to stop everything. Many years of therapy have been a saving grace and now especially with telemedicine. Online therapy session has allowed me not to miss any appointments for two years now. Depression is like a master manipulator twisting everything. When your depression gets so bad you feel like taking your life, I hope you remember you're not alone. Reach out for help. It can get better. It is a daily battle you will fight. Don't give up you are worth it.

❦ At its very worst, my depression takes everything from me - literally everything. I lose my motivation to even roll out of bed to eat. I know my depression has reached full throttle when I begin losing weight without trying to lose weight. In the depths of my depression, I will totally irate myself and cut off all communication. Those who understand me know that there is something drastically wrong if I miss posting to social media for more than 24 hours. Depression is real and it hurts!

❦ At its worst, my depression drowns me. The best way to describe it is a crushing weight that drags me down, like when you're being pulled to the bottom of a pool. I lose any and all will to do everything, even exist some days. Even breathing becomes a chore. My wife, and my close friends, know when to check on me if I stop posting on social media or I leave messages on read for too long. Though I know I'm not alone, my depression pushes the thoughts that I am alone or a burden to the forefront of my mind. It takes time, but I'm usually able to pull myself out, and remind myself that I'm not alone and that it'll be ok. Depression is the silent killer for a reason, but remember you are never alone. It's always darkest just before the dawn.

❦ I was diagnosed with mixed depression and anxiety. The worse of the worlds to me. My depression at times will paralyze or cripple me. What I mean by this is disorders consequences brought on later in life from PTSD. I am an outgoing and in the spotlight individual. I am always going, going and going around lots of people. The human Energizer bunny if you will. When the depression would hit me, prior to medication, I would be solitude, exhausted, a hermit, avoider of any human contact or activities. Then the anxiety part would kick in and I would start feeling I was a letdown, a disappointment to others, a failure. The process repeats itself over and over. These effects would cause me to not want to move out of bed or the couch. Not eat, not bathe, and certainly not communicate with anyone on any platform.

❀ I noticed when my depression gets bad, my eating habits follow along. I barely eat, sleep, or hydrate, but I lay in bed and try and nap which usually ends up with me getting trapped without actually gaining rest. I stay in my room. If I'm hungry when I wake up, I go back to bed until the pain goes away. When I have the resources, I would get crossed or overdo whatever substance I was using to knock myself out so that I wouldn't have to think. In general, I have suicidal ideations, but they seem more probable when depressed. My mind spirals. Fortunately, I know my signs a bit and I try to move around to get my mind off things.

❀ It was bad that I have done a lot of self-destructive behaviors over the year. Even a few suicide attempts. I do have the semicolon tattoo. A semicolon tattoo is a tattoo of the semicolon punctuation mark (;) used as a message of affirmation and solidarity against suicide, depression, addiction, and other mental health issues.

❀ My depression at its worst reaches the point of consistent suicide ideation, ruminating of the past, and asking myself "what's the point of moving forward?" I feel like I fall off the deep end and into self-isolation mode. I'm really struggling with the overturning of Roe v Wade, a series of anti-LGBTQ+ legislation introduced across the country, on top of the endless continuation of the COVID 19 pandemic. I can't help but feel hopeless. Everything seems to keep accumulating simultaneously into an unbearable stream of obstacles. I'm slowly trudging through one of my worst depressive episodes and having a social support system has never been more important. Unfortunately, my best friends & family live across the country. I'm doing my best to make meaningful connections here in Los Angeles, California, United States, but the struggle is real. Aside from self-isolation which feels like a self-fulfilling prophecy. Despite craving friendships, I continue to isolate and feel lonely as hell in doing it. I also struggle with eating and oversleeping. All in all, if you're feeling similar, just know that you are not alone in this rocky journey.

❀ My depression has gotten so bad that I've almost committed suicide. It's a horrible feeling when there's something out there that you can't control. I'm hated by many but loved by many people too. My life changed since the Pulse shooting in Orlando, Florida, United States. I wasn't there but was supposed to be at the bar that night. I wish I would have been there and was killed because since the newspaper came out about me being a Pulse survivor, it crushed my drag world.

❀ Mine ebbs and flows. As a single-parent, I didn't have the "luxury" of being able to stay in bed and disconnect when I was down. The weight of my responsibilities was great. My therapist said that I was highest-functioning depressive she'd ever met. Never late or missed work. Several times, I have had thoughts of suicide, but I have only admitted that to a few people. The negative things I think about myself are unimaginable to anyone that knows me. I rarely socialize and when I do, it takes everything I have in me to leave the house.

❀ Depression can be crippling; physically, emotionally, and mentally. On "good" depression days I can ease the symptoms by a quick little trip to the store (which usually means spending money I do not have, which in turn adds to the depression). On "bad" depression days getting out of bed feels impossible. Knowing I have to get up and function as an adult and a mother makes me sick to my stomach on those days. Depression at its worse for me means pondering if anyone would even notice if I was no longer on this earth.

❀ I was different, I was ostracized at best, badly beaten at worst. When I was 15, I escaped into my music to avoid my unhappiness, and music became tattooed to my soul. I wanted a "gender role reassignment operation." I suffered from a "gender identity crisis." It was a different time, and "homosexuality" was still a psychiatric diagnosis. I struggled. Confusion, therapy, bad relationships. Followed by more confusion, more therapy, and, you got it, more bad relationships. Years into therapy, I was still involved in one bad relationship after another, taking five different psychiatric medications, and very, very unhappy. I became overwhelmed and severely depressed. All too often, I would sleep late into the afternoon. I almost lost my job. Somewhere around the turn of the century, I discovered drag. So, there it was, and it was perfect. I could use my ability to remember song lyrics, my talent to lip sync, and years of perfecting my maleness to become a gender illusionist. I was mistaken for a man time again and again and again.

I used my music and talents to masquerade as a man... and passed successfully. Life was good. What more could I possibly need?

❀ My depression can get to the point where I close all doors and shut everyone out of my life. I just focus on working feeling alone and wanting to talk to someone but feel I can't talk to anyone. One point I attempted to take my life five years ago but survived.

❀ I find myself locked in the house with no visitors, no interest in nothing, or nobody while I waddle in self-pity

❀ When my depression hits at it's worse, I can't eat nor function plus I lack enough energy to do the simplest house chores. I have to force myself to eat so I don't get sick due to my diabetes.

❀ I know it's at its worst when I start thinking about death being a relief. It's almost like I feel it would be a pleasure to pass on, rather than staying alive. It can be pretty bad to where my mental anguish is unbearable. This can range from a "dark cloud" to a "violent tornado" that is inescapable once I'm in its vortex. I also don't want to eat or drink but rather just lay in bed. Household tasks fall to the waste side and my self-care goes into shambles. Even simple things seem impossible and I find myself unable to cope or see anything in a solution-orientated manner. I also end up ruminating on painful things and often times I cry for humanity.

❀ My depression is the debilitating type. It can keep me where I don't want to eat, have no interest in food. I will also lose interest in doing the things I normally love. This means just not caring if I do anything at all. I don't sleep, if I'm lucky I may actually sleep four hours; even then it's restless. I will not want to talk to anyone and just zone out. But it starts slowly and builds, so you don't notice it creeping in.

❀ Depression expresses itself at its worst when I am contemplating the actual steps it takes to unalive myself. When I've gotten so low that in my mind the only relief I can get from all the stressors is to remove myself permanently from the planet, then I know that it's bad. Depression runs in my family and I've lost multiple loved ones to suicide.

❀ My anxiety feeds into my depression and vice versa. Most of it is caused by the environments, the trauma around my learning disabilities and my occupation. At its worst I go into sleep mode where my body shuts down. I can't physically stay awake for more than a couple hours a day. That is a suicide symptom that I did not know was a suicide symptom as it is not normally discussed. When I told my doctor about it, they got me into counselling and help right away. Now I know what to look for and reach out for help before it gets to that stage again. I have never been one with negative thoughts or more than normal thoughts about life and death. People just kept telling me it was ok. They told me I was just tired and if I rested I would be better, since I didn't have thoughts of self-harm or harm to others and was always happy, and finding the positive in life. I am very fortunate to have found the doctor I did who recognized what was happening and got me into the process of finding the help I needed.

❀ My depression has lots of different areas that it comes from- childhood trauma, PTSD, sexual assault, domestic violence, bullying childhood and as an adult; there is probably more. I have planned many ways for me to die. I felt it would just be easier than dealing with my life. I'm disabled, it's called Charcot-Marie-Tooth disease. I also have a habit of shutting everyone out including the ones closest to me. It is a bit of a slow process, so it makes it hard for people to know what's going on. People think my life just got busy. Being a Transgender Man has also been a long road to walk with my depression. I couldn't ask for better help than that I get from my spouse and therapist.

❀ At its worst I isolate and stay in bed, in the dark mostly. I have very little energy. I likely don't eat a whole lot on that day but if I ate, I may not necessarily have the energy to shower. If I got up and showered.

❀ When my depression is at its worse, I can't even get out of bed. I lay in bed in complete darkness. I close up and not talk to anyone.

❀ I know I'm at my worst when I sleep all day. I also have chronic pain and mobility issues and that gets worse too. It's a vicious cycle. I don't want to do the things I need to do in order to take care of myself when I'm at my worst.

❀ I hit a bad day once when I was at my lowest, when my heart got broken. I literally ran after someone who I knew wasn't best for me, fell in the road and cried. I didn't think tail lights could make me so sad. I had to make ends on my own and had my emotional support taken away, whether they were animals that I shared an emotional attachment with or otherwise. My money reached an all-time low so I was unable to make ends meet and pay bills. I worked an 8 am to 9 pm job that made me feel like a number. They would not have noticed if I was gone. All these things stacked like building blocks pushing me further down until I could see no more light.

❀ Being a performer with severe depression whose made it through multiple attempts on my life, this is a question that hits home. When my depression is at its worst, I don't want to do anything. For example, even the littlest things like brushing my hair and teeth are hard to accomplish. I also notice my depression can completely stop any creative idea from passing through my brain. The worst depression though has sent me to the hospital to recover. The hospitals are the only reason I am still here today.

❀ My depression can get pretty bad. I have autism, attention-deficit/hyperactivity disorder (ADHD), PTSD, and anxiety along with depression and none of those were treated when I was a child. I spent most of my life trying to navigate a world that is set up against me and it was traumatic. I often feel numb and worthless. I feel like nothing will ever get better and I feel like I contribute no value to this world.

❀ My depression is one of the many symptoms of my severe PTSD. I have been through over ten years of therapy to learn to cope and I am better; my depression still likes to slip in occasionally. When it's at its worse, it effects my dissociative identity disorder (D.I.D). When I am unable to cope during my depression dips, my disorder takes over. That is when I know I'm hitting depression super hard. Most of the time I can pull out of it in time, but sometimes it lasts for weeks.

❀ I remember waking up in the Emergency Room. I was pretty hazy. Had I been? Where? I felt myself fade. "We're losing her! Get the paddles! FAST!" "Your so-called friends left you here to die!" "… admitted Tuesday…. Stomach pump… Didn't wake up until late Friday night…" I woke up listening to the night nurse. I couldn't speak. I couldn't breathe. I grunted. I hurt. Did I get beat up again? Felt like I'd been beat up again. My mind was so dull. Crying, strapped down, and alone, I was thinking, Why can't they fix me? Don't they know this isn't who I'm supposed to be? How could God mess up something like this? Don't they know my mind doesn't match up with the rest of me, and the rest of me doesn't match up with much of anything? Had I really told them I wanted to get the operation? Who did I tell? Did I take that whole bottle of pills? Who knew? I don't want to live if I can't be who I really am. Do I have to die to make them understand? Why can't they understand that I almost died trying to become who I really am?

❀ Sometimes it can get pretty isolating and lonely. I've found when I'm not performing as often are the times, I get deeper into depression!

❀ At its worst; I've literally woken up in a tub of hot water with razor marks with Emergency Medical Technician's resuscitating me. But more recently, I've only been in seclusion from everyone and everything. My dog often helps me too.

❀ My depression can get so bad to the point that I have a complete meltdown and can't stop shaking uncontrollably.

❀ My depression has gotten so bad I have attempted suicide four times. If it does not get that far I usually mostly sleep and completely shut down and don't eat or drink.

❀ When I feel myself going into a depressive state, I put all of my energy and focus into my stage persona. It's my own personal escape from the "real world" at times. Realistically, I know I'm the same person. Mentally, my drag puts me in a completely different headspace. It's something that I created on my own terms with my own rules and no one can take that away from me, because it is me.

❀ At its worst, my depression has made me question my worth and whether I should even be alive and whether anyone cares. It truly felt like no one could understand my specific circumstances. I have lots of trauma in my past and as I heal from it over time, both with and without the help of others, I struggle to remind myself to keep up the work I do both for myself and my community. I've gone into intensive care units during the pandemic for mental health treatment because I was a danger to myself and could not hold myself accountable to keeping myself alive. My partner was very worried. I had isolated myself from my loved ones because I didn't think people would understand.

❀ At my worst, I completely shut out the world. I stop engaging with people. I stop caring about my obligations, which results in my performance at work rapidly tanking. It takes every ounce of energy I have to even show up to work, and it becomes impossible for me to arrive on time. I struggle to continue doing what is necessary for survival as little more than an empty shell on autopilot. I don't become suicidal in the way that most people associate with that term, actively trying to end my life. Rather, I become suicidal in the more general, subtle way of no longer caring if I live.

❀ At my worst, I see every single flaw on my body. I think to myself, I'll never be the man I'm striving to be in life. No matter how many pull ups I can do, no matter how much time I spend at the gym. Those are the times when I briefly think about breaking my 37-year sobriety. Luckily, I never do.

❀ Recently I've started going to a dark place. To the point that I'm now seeking help. Drag is a good outlet, uplifting.

❀ When I was at my lowest, I was suicidal. I lost counts how many times. At age 47 started my transitioning to the man I am today and those thoughts have vanished. Main reason because I found myself, my voice. I am not saying there aren't days I struggle still because I do, but now I withdraw and find my inner peace before I react.

❀ My depression at its worst is when I'm feeling not worthy, second guessing what I'm doing, losing faith and being in my head too much. I begin feeling like a pressure cooker.

❀ My depression is low-key. Drag gives me affirmation that I'm not alone and that people like what I do.

❀ At its worse I could only think of ways to kill myself. I felt worthless. Life was throwing normal problems, mostly financial, making it worse and added to the emotional disconnect.

❀ I was diagnosed with Major Depressive Disorder and Anxiety at seventeen years of age, and after I had long realized I was transgender. I was a cutter by the age of twelve and have been suicidal many times in my life. It was only after I discovered the art of Drag that I found my sanctuary. The stage is where I always share a part of my story, reveal parts of my true self, and find purpose again. Drag saved my life, and it has allowed me to help others living in a darkness that at times, nearly swallowed me whole.

❀ My depression can get so bad I don't even get out of bed and stay in a dark room. I find myself often crying.

❀ At its worst I've found myself facing down the barrel of a gun or cutting my wrist. It got pretty dark.

❀ I get to the point where I don't eat because I don't think I deserve it. I lay on bed feeling guilty about my existence. I feel like my friends and family would do better without me. Just sitting in the dark with the thoughts for hours.

❀ My depression is a constant presence in my life. At its worst, it renders me incapable of daily activity and prevents me from seeing any beauty or worth within myself.

❀ Depression is chaotic. I feel as I am curled up tightly and cry hysterically. The worse comes out of me when it happens. I feel totally alone. The energy is not there when depression hits the hardest.

❀ For me depression is an everyday battle. It's a fight that I have to conquer every day. At my best I can laugh and spend time around people. At my worst I lay in bed unable to eat and go into a sort of coma where I don't remember parts of my day.

❀ I just want to get away from everyone and everything when my depression gets to its worse. I just cuddle with my velour pillow and sleep 18-22 hours to escape... usually on the weekend when I don't have to work.

❀ When I'm depressed, it nearly always coincides with my anxiety and ADHD. I constantly worry about the worst things happening, and my ADHD speeds that worry up. There's so much I'm worried about, I nearly cry every time that I get to my worst. I constantly worry that I will never achieve what I want to in my life. I automatically start to wonder what the purpose of living is if I never can achieve my dreams.

❀ For me my depression gets to the point of not eating and sleeping, but at the same time hyper focusing on projects just to burn myself out. At this point I end up barely talking and just "zoning out" for most of the time.

Chapter Two, Question Two
"When do you realize that your depression
is not just feeling down for a moment?"

❀If I am feeling down, I surround myself with people that make me happy. When I am depressed, I push them away. It is truly that simple.

❀ When it just keeps continuing and nothing relieves it; not performing, shopping or cuddling with my dog.

❀ When I have isolated myself from others. It usually takes a couple of months for me to get to this point.

❀ You realize when the feelings you experience begin to become daily or your common normal. Everything that happens around you seems to begin to reflect the feelings you're experiencing. It can also be when you start physically not feeling well, as depression can and will lower your energy as well as lowers your immune system causing even more problems which can unfortunately even further prolong depressive episodes.

❀ I realize when I finally eat or grab a shower and go, "Umm, I think I forgot to eat for a few days."

❀ PTSD is really true and a big deal. I kept busy, juggling two to three jobs at a time, including DRAG. The horror of my childhood still haunts me today. I was shunned all my life for being gay. I was sexually molested as a child by my step-father. It continued until I was a teenager. I ran away from home.

❀ I realized it when I noticed I would spend literally weeks in bed at a time sleeping, sobbing and honestly losing track of any concept of time. My emotions were rampant and uncontrollable.

❀ I don't always notice it until I'm on the other side. It becomes almost normal for me to feel so down. It's not until the fog starts to lift and I attempt to rejoin the world that I realize it was bad. I realize I'm in a funk, fully self-isolating or self-sabotaging, which only makes it worse.

❀ My Mother had been diagnosed with Manic depression when I was little. Back in those days they prescribed Lithium and what was called by people, Black Beauty's. They gave her white crosses to keep energy levels higher. Being a young child, I was told that I had melancholy. I had contacted Child Protective Services (CPS) at my school many times for the abuse but they would never talk to me, and my parents just told them I was overly emotional! One CPS worker set up an appointment with a child therapist and within one visit, I was diagnosed with melancholy and mania. My teacher told me that she did not believe it because she was more a mother to me then my own. Around age ten, after my parents' punishment of sewing needles jabbed into my legs and a day in the hall closet under lock and key, I told my teacher. I was taken to the hospital and after hours of treatment for my wounds and malnutrition, the wonderful Doctor brought in an Adult Psychiatrist who diagnosed me with what was called Shell shock. It was a name given mostly to the soldiers coming back from War. Today it is called PTSD. The medications they gave me helped, but the sad thing is they put me right back in with my parents and the story continued. I realized then that I was damaged goods. I just did not realize it was severe depression until I was much older.

❀ When all my drag ends up packed away.

❀ When I buy items for a creative outfit and then lose motivation to create the project. I end up either wearing plain everyday clothes or not even going to the show.

❀ I'm going to state current experience rather than past. For me it's realizing I haven't read in days. I know a show is weeks away yet haven't started on it. I get up for work so late that I barely have enough time to go to work. The one that made me realize it the most was in the winter I feel exhausted. I jumped at every chance to leave the house even though I have to deal with crowds and noise. Leaving meant I might run away from feeling so tired for five minutes. I go to the store knowing it will mess with my sensory issues, overwhelming me with sounds, which is an amazing idea because it's better than feeling like nothing.

❀ My depression started in my adolescence. I was told for years that it was just puberty. It wasn't just a normal teen thing when I started feeling suicidal. Unfortunately, it took the people and doctors around me when I was eighteen to realize that I had clinical depression. In terms of recognizing when an episode starts, my warning signs are I get irritable and start to either oversleep or lose sleep. I also find my eating disorder flares up and I lose motivation.

❀ I know that my depression has kicked in when I stop posting on social media and lose my appetite!

❀ I usually don't realize until I start to get better or someone intervenes. In the moment, it makes sense to me.

❀ I notice when I would spend days in bed sleeping or just crying because I didn't know where my life was going. I would skip meals and conversations with friends or family. I just felt like I didn't have any energy to do anything.

❀ I realize it when my mind continues to go out of sorts. When performing, family, crafts and other things I love just isn't snapping me back into reality. Then I know I have to figure out what will actually help and relieve what is going on and what actually caused it. Sometimes it takes a short period of time; other times it can take months to snap out of it.

❀ I can usually tell my depression is coming on stronger because my anxiety begins to build. I start feeling panicked and then my energy severely drops.

❀ When you don't know anything other than the depression and it consumes your life.

❀ When you're so sad and depressed daily. You can't stop thinking about yourself and wanting to end all of it.

❀ I can tell the difference between sadness and depression when the feelings of impending doom take over. It feels like there is a heavy weight on my being and no matter what I try to do, it cannot be shaken, so, I just stop trying. I fight every day just to roll over and get up out of bed.

❀ I know my depression is kicking in when I don't want to get out of bed. Besides suffering with depression, I have terrible fibromyalgia and arthritis. That only adds to my depression. I will lay in bed wondering why do I have to suffer in pain or can't I just die. I don't want to do anything or see anyone. Once I come out of my depression, I want to do all kind of fun stuff and push myself to the limits.

❀ I know all my senses and emotions quiet well. Sadness or feeling down is an in and out type of feeling. When depression creeps in, it's like a tsunami and it envelopes everything about me and my functions.

❀ That's always hard to tell, but usually for me it can actually physically hurt. Usually that's the "oh shit" moment where I am hiding and crying.

❀ My depression came on slowly I didn't realize that it was depression, I just thought the world sucked. I thought happy people were blessed and I was a mistake. Born to suffer. The US Marine Corps helped me get courage and confidence to examine my issues to myself. I ran far and fast away from my true identity. I am a retired, wounded veteran. I couldn't do my either of my chosen professions when I started healing from brain damage. I felt worthless. I thought there was no room in the world for me. And I felt like a ghost.

❀ My depression came fast and hard. It is continuous.

❀ I know almost immediately when my depression isn't temporary because I've gotten quite familiar with my depressive triggers and symptoms over the years. I essentially experience a prolonged period of feeling extremely low. In my experience everything goes dark, even if the sun is shining bright, my brain translates every moment into a dark tainted memory. I start to experience sounds differently; I also no longer experience the same excitement with things that would typically bring me joy such as Drag. Everything turns dull. I also experience severe irritability in each depressive episode to the point where I feel "on edge" all the time. I often get caught in a loop which I call the "I'm over it" mode. I feel like I want to mentally and physically check out until I can break free from this overwhelming agony. Then of course, the self-isolation symptom appears which essentially strips me from my social identity, as a result, I cancel plans with friends left and right, and lock myself in my room.

❀ I realize when my depression is not a down moment when I start to cry and start thinking suicidal thoughts that's when it's gone too far. I have coping skills that I use like walking, listening to music and or writing in a journal. Doing drag has helped me with my depression and other illnesses.

❀ I have struggled with depression long enough to know my own symptoms, how my body reacts, how my mind plummets. Usually, it shows up in the form of extreme lethargy. I lay around in bed, making myself more miserable by not doing anything I know I like doing, won't eat, won't take care of myself and/or my plants, won't talk to or see anyone. When I do realize this for what it is, it can be incredibly hard still to tell myself, "You will feel better if you just get up." I literally just watch the sunset and make myself even more depressed because I love the sunshine and I missed all of it. I stress about how I got nothing done and it makes it worse. I find myself repeating 'just get up. Once you're up you'll be able to start the steps to feel better' but sometimes I just really can't get up. Once it hits a few days of this constantly, that definitely solidifies that it is my depression coming back for a visit and not just my being upset in the moment. You can certainly be upset for something for a long while, without it necessarily being depression. We are all humans that can feel depressed.

❀ It usually takes a day or two. It's when I find myself engaging in "all or nothing" thinking and behaviors, or when I suddenly crave only really bland, beige food you might give to a small child when they're ill. That and the coldness, I feel cold when it's a proper depressive episode.

❀ I was always the guy that said "get over it" or "what do you have to be depressed about?" I didn't think depression was real… until it happened to me. My birthdays have always been a terrible time for me. Through therapy, I learned that it goes all the way back to birthday party my parents planned when I was in second grade. It was the typical kids party, inviting everyone from school. Not one person showed up. It was my 49th birthday when I sat at Iguana Mia, alone, getting my free birthday dinner, that the suicidal thoughts were nearly unbearable. The next morning, I reached out for help. I couldn't leave my young son alone that way.

❀ It takes a while for me to realize it's a depression episode since I'm on medication. But everything starts to bring me down, even compliments. At the point that I realize it's depression, I've already managed to convince myself that people are just trying to be nice or polite and not meaning anything positive that they say.

❀ Depression for me seemed to start in middle school… although I did not know what was depression. I was often told I was just "moody" or being dramatic when I would cry and shut down from everyone. I was not diagnosed with depression clinically until 2010 when I lost my father to colon cancer. After going to a grief counselor, we realized I had been struggling with depression for many years!

❀ I kind of always had depression, at least since I was seven years old. Going to college was when my depression took a dive for the worst. Depression isn't just being sad, it's ruthless. It makes you feel like you are the only human on earth, even when in a crowded room. It makes doing anything, even showering, feel like a chore.

❀ I try to be mindful of how long I've been in the state for. It can be challenging at first but I've trained myself to observe my thoughts and feelings and when I'm in a dark state, I keep track of how long I'm in it. I also try to see if I can move out of it, with time. When I can't, that's when I'm in the danger zone. I'm also very prone to suicidal ideation and I notice when the intensity goes up (once again by mindfully observing my thoughts) past a certain point, then I'm in the danger zone. I know I'm past that point when I've pushed past passive ideation and into active ideation. This looks like day dreaming about doing it (with an intent), formulating a plan (how I would do it) and then taking concrete steps towards doing it. If I get to that point, then I know I'm in trouble and need help because I'm not succeeding in staying safe by myself.

❀ When I notice that I've disconnected from people I talk to all the time. I'm a talker and when I don't talk to anyone for days.

❀ It usually takes me about three or four days to realize that the depression is not just a momentary thing. As the days go by it slowly deescalates but it's very slow.

❀ The realization doesn't really sink in until about a week in, when nothing in life is making me happy. Not my child. Not my dogs. Not my cats. The things I do that always bring me joy in life will bring me nothing.

❀ When you have all the blessings that life can give you would expect to look in the mirror and see a glowing person. Time after time I would look in the mirror and see a cold shell. In my head I would scream, "Why can't you be happy why? Why aren't you happy? You have everything physically and emotionally that many seek. I buried my depression in my successes to keep it hidden. I accepted the fact this isn't something I can fight off like a cold. Depression literally was eating me alive. I've been medicated. The current cocktail is Adderall XR, Adderall Instant, Welbutrin and Seroquel. But I always have an excuse to not further my treatment. I would say, I don't have time to lay on a couch and talk to a stranger. These last six months have had me in a car five hours daily and given me plenty of time to think and self-reflect. I am pretty certain now that having that coach will help me continue my battle so I ultimately control the war. Key take away, it's ok to be sad for a day, a week, or even a month, but if after 30 days you can't shake the fog don't be like me and wait years and years thinking you can do it alone. You can't beat depression alone. If you are stuck in the dark place, please know you are loved and wanted. All of us sharing our experiences have been through the trails and we want to live so you can live as well.

❀ The realization doesn't kick in until a few days to a week. That's when I start noticing I'm backing away from everything, being less social, not eating, losing the lack of interest for anything and everything. Sometimes it's not as sever, but other times it gets pretty sever.

❀ I realize my depression is not just feeling down when I am not doing the things that I love or that help others for more than a week. I have learned to give myself a week to process and work through things that may trigger depression episodes. If I don't see improvements within a week, I seek out professional help.

❀ It can be really hard at times; often my spouse and my therapist help me.

❀ I lose interest in music. Music has been my light through the majority of my mental health struggles. I know it's getting worse When I no longer feel like listening to music. It is no longer just a "down for the moment" kind of situation.

❀ I have suffered from depression since I was a child. Currently I have a therapist and a psychiatrist for my severe depression, severe anxiety, and PTSD. There is no shame in seeking help. I also have my wonderful chosen family to lean on when times are difficult.

❀ When I realized, I didn't want to do the things that I would normally bend over backwards to do that gave me joy. Whether it be creating art or spending time with my family and friends. I was unable to respond and would lay in my bed unable to move; like I was being tied down by a ton of bricks. My heart felt tight and hurt. I felt like I was looking out a window while the world was still turning and time was frozen around me.

❀ Once it's been a few days or weeks of feeling bad, I'm in a depressive episode, but it can be hard to recognize in the moment. I have other mental health issues that coincide with the depression I've been dealing with my whole life.

❀ When I realized dad wanted a boy. He had me out in the backyard shirtless so he could pretend I was his son. Not daughter. He used to say to folks, "If it's a girl I'll just drown it in the Ohio river and fix that shit." That's where it all began.

❀ I realize my depression has officially hit when I do not feel like doing anything at all. I feel this overwhelming feel of dread, self-hatred, and feel like nothing I do will ever be enough. I realize my depression takes its gnarly hold of my brain when even the small things that normally make me smile, like a new piece of jewelry or a new song dropping from my favorite artist, no longer makes that smile come across my face.

❀ I realized that my depression was not just feeling down for a moment during my only year of four-year college. During the 2016-2017 school year, I was not myself and no one noticed. I stopped going to classes, I spent most of my time in my room in bed with the TV playing in the background to drown out the sound of silence.

❀ There is a complete lack of motivation; my interests don't seem interesting to me. The closest feeling I could say is completely burned out.

❀ I know when my dissociative identity disorder (DID) acts up, that my depression is bad. Leading up to me losing control, I feel extremely down, lethargic, and unmotivated. When I start losing time frames of certain days, then I know that my disorder has kicked in. That only happens when my depression isn't just a "moment."

❀ I started to have night terrors when I was in college. I was suffering from a great deal of grief and loss. I had lost family member after family member and then Hurricane Katrina. I did not have time to process any of it. After several months of vivid night terrors, I realized I needed help. I was fortunate enough to have a school counselor. Just talking about what happened with someone really helped with the healing process.

❀ About a week into it is when I usually notice that I am starting to slip down that slide of depression! Usually starts with me being exhausted from too much at once. I isolate myself and after about a week if I'm not feeling better, I know that I'm going to be struggling with depression.

❀ When I have for weeks or months at a time tucked away by secluding myself from everyone and everything. I do not realize how much time I've been hiding.

❀ I will detach and isolate more and more. My emotions will be all over the place. I self-assess as soon as I notice I am feeling hopeless.

❀ When nothing or nobody, not even my pets can cheer me up or make me smile. That's when I know that I am depressed and not just sad or feeling down.

❀ Normally I don't realize it. It just hits me. I'm sure I could look for more signs but most of the time I just don't try to. I push myself to the breaking point most times before I do anything about it.

❀ I tend to convince myself that my depressive states are just feeling a bit down. I downplay much of what I go through mentally, so it doesn't affect anyone else. I have many friends who struggle with many different severities of depression, luckily mine is very infrequent. When it's here… it's here! I throw myself into my stage work and craft and build myself back up mentally.

❀ I know I am in a deep stage of depression when I allow everything to pass me by. I don't feel like I'm living life just being a part of it. I sometimes have outer body experience where I can see everything just happening and I can't react to it until I just break down and cry.

❀ I feel withdrawn. Not only do I have loss of interest in being around people, but I start to feel irritated when I am around someone. That has nothing to do with who they are or our relationship. Mood swings are also drastic and irrational. My depression doesn't come in the form of sadness all the time. I get extremely angry at things that I might normally consider a mild annoyance. I start crying when I watch or read something sweet and adorable. I become far more sensitive to sensory input and reach 'overload' far more quickly. Depression is complicated; that's why it can be so hard to recognize, especially by those who haven't experienced it.

❀ I realize that my depression is not just feeling down for a moment usually the longevity of the feeling. When it felt like there was not anything I can do to bring myself out of it and the things I usually enjoy don't have their usual effect in terms of making me happy to be alive. My first signs of being depressed are usually an inability to eat and an increasing feeling of hopelessness. It's like my body moves all things that make life worth living to the back burner: sex, food, time with friends, enjoying my hobbies. I end up feeling that the world is awful and the agony involved is insurmountable and its endless and will never change.

❀ When I feel a certain way for more than a short period of time and I can't figure out what's going on and I can't shake the emotions.

❀ When you lose track of days and it doesn't matter what you've done well, all you dwell is on is the issues at hand.

❀ When I realized the darkness of depression seemed to follow me everywhere then I knew it was not simply a low point that would pass. It became a daily struggle trying to find happiness and a motivation to keep going. Discovering Drag opened a door that allowed me to explore everything I never knew about myself and find out who I am, who I was meant to be and where I fit in this world.

❀ ❀ When I didn't want to get out if bed or didn't enjoy what usually brought me pleasure.

❀ The first time I cut myself and didn't feel any regrets.

❀ When PTSD hit! Tried suicide for first time... I took pills and alcohol. I was found and almost died three times on way to hospital.

❀ I think I realized my depression was more than feeling down when I was a kid. Others around me would feel down for a little bit, and I'd see them get out of their funk and dust it off like it was nothing! I would stay in that "funk" for days or weeks. It just didn't make any sense to me until I was later diagnosed with depression and anxiety as a teenager.

❀ When I was younger, I wanted to make the "pain" stop, it wasn't physical but I knew I was hurting deep. I didn't know how to describe it. I felt like my existence was a burden, nothing mattered.

❀ I realize that my depression is encompassing when I find myself completely incapable of performing regularly daily or mundane tasks. From showering to even leaving the house, depression renders me unable to function.

❀ The moment I realize I'm not just feeling down is when I pull myself away from even the people I love. Usually even if I'm down I'll talk to my friends but if I'm depressed, I get irritated and snap on the people I care about.

❀ I realize that I'm not just feeling down when I ignore all my phone calls and messages from everyone. They say to me, "Why are you ignoring me?"

❀ Many people think depression is just being sad, but it's much more complicated than that. Being depressed is a deep sadness that won't go away because of actual chemical reactions in the brain that happen in people with depression that don't happen in others. For me, when I'm just sad, I'm still somewhat happy and hopeful because I want to go right to my friends for comfort. But when I'm depressed, I just want to keep to myself in my room and not talk to anyone. I feel like there's nothing I can do about it, and I just have to ride it out until it goes away the next morning. It's a sort of feeling hopelessness, as opposed to just being sad.

Chapter Three, Question Three
"Did you think DRAG would help you with
your depression before you began doing DRAG?"

❀ I wanted it to be the cure. I thought the audience would get me out of my head, but I learned something along the way. I realized it is a patch. One tool in my box to fight depression. I won't say one tool because getting ready for a show distracts me. Practicing for a show distracts me. Listening to a song wondering how I would perform it is therapeutic. I never realized so many steps in DRAG could help me. When I am depressed, I forget these moments. This book is making me think things through.

❀ I do think drag would have helped me manage my depression. Before I started performing, I was often unmotivated and didn't want to do much of anything. After the first time I hit the stage, I felt an overwhelming joy I had not felt in a long time. I met my drag family. Between the drag family, fellow performers, and the connections I've made, I've found a support system I never thought I'd have in life.

❀ I don't think I thought of drag being able to help me with my depression. I was in survival mode when I started. It was more of an outlet, an escape, a chance to do something totally different than my normal day to day involvements and it was a space to be creative again without borders. Looking back, it definitely helped and gave me a supportive community that helped take the edge off the depression that was being caused by other issues and trauma. In some cases, some of my numbers helped me work through things that were part of the depression.

❀ Thirty years ago, when I started, drag was fun and frivolous. It brought me joy. As my career grew and I commanded the largest stage in my area, I accumulated a lot of fans and "drag friends". The fans, which I love with all my heart, aren't there when the spotlight is dark. You're a superstar every Saturday night, but eating ice cream on the couch alone all week. It's the same with the community of entertainers here. For many years I hosted the largest variety show in the area and all of the queens around were my best friends. I gave new queens their start, I allowed established queens to share my stage and I opened doors for so many when there were none. When my club finally closed, after 30+ years, none of those entertainers gave me a second thought or considered including me in anything they had going on at their clubs. Drag became a source of pain and a reminder of just how alone I am in the world. "Friends" and "love" should not be conditional, but in the world of entertainment they seem to be. Drag is therapy, though. The music you choose can help tell your story and help you work things out in your head through performing. A song from 1989 that has literally saved my life and still inspires me when I'm down is "I Can't Complain" by Patti LaBelle...listen to lyrics from beginning to end and you'll see.

❀ It wasn't a question when I started. Doing Drag started more as a dare in a talent show. However, once I started, I soon realized that I was happier and felt more at home on the stage. I think knowing I am making other people happy by entertaining them in return brought me joy. It still does!

❀ I do believe drag does help with depression. At times it can be the reason for your depression, and it can make you feel like a failure not only to yourself, but to others.

❀ Drag definitely helps my depression in some ways. Drag helped me start to explore my gender identity, and is part of how I realized I'm nonbinary. I have much more love for myself and how I look in life.

❀ Drag helped me before I became a queen. It helped me become comfortable in the environment, prepare myself for the stage and the anxiety that can come with performing. I also met and learned from many performers before doing drag myself. It built bonds that have lasted through shady times when other performers didn't like me due to my depressed nature I'd sometimes exhibit.

❀ That wasn't something I was thinking about, but it definitely does. When I have a deadline for projects and something to look forward to that helps. It's a great outlet for me that lets me utilize all sorts of my creativity and I'm grateful for it every day.

❀ I did think drag would help. In drag I am not my off-stage person. Someone that was shy, not outgoing. I have an anxiety filled heart every time everyone's eyes on were on me as a public speaker. The one everyone called stupid and blamed everything wrong on. Doing drag and being on stage I was someone else who was the douche bag rocker that chicks want in every movie. I was a totally different person.

❀ I had no idea that it would help with my depression, but I'm so glad it did help me.

❀ I did not think drag in particular would help with my depression before I did it. I'm just an artist and a creative in general, so it wasn't exactly an end goal to dress up and get on stage and assume that I would suddenly no longer be depressed. The lack of motivation to do any art certainly was literally killing me though. I knew that as long as I was able to get back into creating, I would feel better. That has been my entire life, and it will continue to be the rest of my life. It is ingrained deeply into who I am as a person. My tagline is even 'Living Art.' Drag is a subset of my artistic skills. Making costumes, wigs, songs, doing makeup, choreography, and telling a story is an important part of pulling me out of that dark useless cloud I feel when depressed though. Creating anything is the best time I feel alive.

❀ I actually had no idea that drag would help me this much. I knew it would help with my depression just a bit. Drag has become a healthy outlet to express myself and gives me a chance to leave my problems behind me.

❀ Going to drag shows always boosted my mood, even before I started my drag career. The longer I went, the more obvious it was that I had to try it myself. However, depression and my inner demons prevented me from actually starting for a while. It's hard to let your positive feelings outweigh your depressing ones, but the drag community embraced me and helped me find my inner strength.

❀ I had no idea it would help. I thought it would make it worse since I'd have so much work to do with no willpower to do it. I felt better after I went on stage and for several days after I performed.

❀ Drag is what gave me the ability to finally be me. It still helps me today. Because of drag, I can step away from myself and be someone else for short periods of time, a mental vacation from myself when life gets to be too much.

❀ I had no idea drag would help my depression or my anxiety before I began. When I did start and made the connections, I had no idea that I would meet so many people who struggle the same as me. Drag has helped me with my depression in the sense that I have a support group that understands my mind and the way it works. My anxiety has reduced so much since I began to express myself on stage. Being able to talk and keep conversation and the gain of confidence has increased as well.

❀ At first, I didn't think drag would help with my depression but as I continued to do drag the more I found my depression at an ease. Drag has helped me in so many ways, needless to say drag saved my life.

❀ Drag was kind of a toss-up. I figured it would either help or with the constant upkeep of drag would make the depression worse. All in all, it did more "good than harm" for my depression as well as doing wonders to push the boundaries of my social anxieties. It gives me something to look forward to that keeps my spirits up. It gives me a platform to perform music that aligns with how I may be feeling in the moment to release all the pent-up negativity in a positive way. It lets my community know they aren't alone and that someone out there understands what they may be feeling.

❀ I didn't think about it. I know sometimes certain drag situations make my anxiety worse. However, I also have an amazing group of friends to support me.

❀ I thought it would help because I knew I needed things to do and focus on. I didn't realize it would be an ongoing and huge part of my life though.

❀ Creativity always helps with my depression. I didn't consciously go into drag with that goal in mind. I do think it was an influence of finding a new way to express myself. It helped to have something to focus on.

❀ I started drag as part of a fun contest and fundraiser with the Mardi Gras Organization. I had no idea I would find my happy place, my place of peace, my second family. Most drag kings can dance and really preform; I often joke the other king in my group is the "get in your pants king" with his performance, and I am the "get in your heart king." I tend to perform to songs that will make you think or tug at your heart strings... ultimately this is the way I get all my raw emotions out. This is why drag helps with my depression, I can be 100% pure and honest, yet hide behind my stage name. Drag is life change for me and has opened my eye and many other's eyes as well to major issues we in the LGBTQ+ world face daily.

❀ I honestly didn't know if it would work on me. It was a wonderful surprise when I figured out that it did work. I love to entertain an audience. It is an amazing unexplainable moment for me to temporarily become the person I created.

❀ I didn't understand the freedom of truly being myself.

❀ The entire reason I started doing drag is because a friend of mine, who was hosting a drag competition, asked me if I'd be a contestant. After rudely reminding her that I wasn't interested in doing drag, she explained the possibility of bookings for the next six months. When I was still hesitant, she stated that I had been going through some things and needed something to keep my mind busy and distracted. She suggested that it would give me something to look forward to doing. I had just come home from four months of mental health treatment (two months out-patient in my home state, and two months in patient halfway across the country).

❀ I knew DRAG would help me. I needed an outlet and knew it would give me the chance to be anyone but myself for five minutes at a time.

❀ I had not realized I was clinically depressed before I started doing drag at 21. I just realized I felt pretty in drag...even as a 'big' girl.

❀ I didn't believe anything could help me. I didn't believe I had anything in me worth saving. I needed community and family, and as an anxious, depressed, traumatized and neurodiverse person I can feel really awkward and uncomfortable in clubs and at events. Performing, promoting, volunteering always allowed me to participate and connect whilst having a purpose to anchor myself in. Performing gave me access to community, which gave me strength and support. Performing gave me purpose, which gave me confidence. Most importantly, drag let me explore gender, which I didn't know I needed, but over the years allowed me to explore, unpack and come to terms with my own transness. I would never have known how much of my trauma and depression was tied to my dysphoria if I hadn't found euphoria in drag.

❀ Honestly, I didn't expect drag to have such an impact on me. I wasn't sure what I thought when I decided to take the stage for the first time. I'm just so grateful that it gave me life, a voice and an outlet that has ultimately saved me on many levels. It has helped with almost every aspect of my life from depression, to self-acceptance.

❀ Yes, absolutely! I knew Drag had the capacity to mitigate the severity of my depressive symptoms. However, not to the extent that it actually did! Drag has literally saved my life multiple times and continues to give me a reason to keep plowing forward; I'm so lucky that I discovered this passion at such a pivotal moment in my life. I came out as nonbinary about a year before I became infatuated with this art-form, I was also going through a really difficult breakup at the time so I intuitively knew that things were going to get better once I was able to step on that stage. The trajectory of my life completely changed!

❀ I didn't know what to expect from drag when I started. I had only seen one drag show ever at that point. I guess I knew having found my people would bring some relief, but I didn't expect it to be the outlet its became in my life.

❀ No, I didn't. I fell into drag by accident. I didn't realize how much it would change my life when I first started. I may only do two numbers per show but for those six to eight minutes, I get to forget about my problems and be someone that doesn't have a care in the world.

❀ Actually, I didn't realize it would change my life. I started doing Drag because I was offered a part as a Drag Queen for a movie being filmed in New Orleans and I didn't want to look silly and ignorant. Long story short, I fell in love with Drag and I started to love myself for the first time in my life.

❀ When I started doing drag it was to get out of the house on the weekend. Little did I know at the time how therapeutic it would be for me in the long term! The friends I have made over the years have weathered every storm life has cast my way.

❀ When I started drag, I had no idea what it would do for my life. I started because I saw my male friends all dressing as queens. I always wondered where the male representation was, so I decided to put on that face and rock out. Little did I know, that would open up a whole bunch of questions about my own gender and lead to me transitioning! I swear without drag and without my little family of drag performers, I don't know where I would be today but I know for a fact that it saved my life.

❀ I did see drag as something that could potentially help my mental health which is part of the reason I started. It gives me an outlet to truly express myself which is what I needed.

❀ I started to do drag a few years after my depression was alleviated and my mood became stabilized. I believe that if I had maybe done it when I was depressed, it would have given me something to feel good about and have a way to express myself in a better way.

❀ Yes. Drag helped when my depression was high. Just being able to be around the other performers and the audience who would come and see you perform helped me.

❀ When I first started drag, it was to bring me out of my introverted ways. I believed drag gave me the power to be and do anything. I use drag many times to pull me out of depression. Most of the time it works. Drag has helped me beyond any therapy I have ever done. It has far exceeded my expectations.

❀ I was very outgoing with no shame before my depression hit hard in middle school. I never cared what others said or thought. I became insecure with myself through the years of having depression. When I started drag, I just came out nonbinary and wanted to break the cycle. I wanted to be more secure with myself and play around to see if I would be comfortable more as male. Drag has helped me cope with so much more than my gender identity. It's more like a therapy session for me. It helped me become my authentic self.

❀ I honestly didn't think there would be a connection between doing DRAG and my depression. Once I got a few performances under my belt, I began to realize that DRAG was an activity that helps release dopamine in my brain and that the "rush" of the show makes me feel good.

❀ I did not think drag would help with my depression, but it absolutely has helped me. Having a creative outlet is always very therapeutic for me and beneficial to my mental health.

❀ Actually? No. I had no idea that drag would end up being so good for my depression. I had a long history in theater previous to entering the world of drag, so I knew that drag would be fun. It wasn't until after I started doing drag that I realized that it has helped me hold my deep depression at bay. Drag has been a tremendous help to me and given me outlets to escape my real world, even if it's for the length of most songs.

❀ Absolutely not. I didn't even correlate the two of them. Five and half years later, now it's a totally different story as drag is part of my self-therapy.

❀ My depression and anxiety disorder didn't start until well into my drag career when I found out the man who, after finding out I was gay and living with my partner at that time, called me a faggot, was having an affair. This man was my father, who had raised me in a very strict Pentecostal upbringing. Church three to four times a week and rules upon rules and to follow the bible period. This caused such a whirlwind of confusion that I later, due to allowing my depression to fester, I developed PTSD and had to seek professional help and begin a daily medication. Today I can say my therapy and medication have turned my life around drastically!

❀ I wasn't sure if it would help me, but I knew that performing would help me. I was a go-go dancer before doing drag. Even though I had only been dancing for a year, I knew that being up on stage and looking my fear and anxiety in the face would help me to tremendously overcome it.

❀ I never thought drag would ever help me with depression or anxiety. Honestly, I was surprised it didn't make it worse. I was always rather shy and didn't want to draw attention to myself. All through school I would get anxiety even reading in a class with ten to thirty other students. Even now, the idea that being in the spotlight on a stage could help me, blows my mind.

❀ I was able to understand at that time. It did help as time went on.

❀ I had no idea it would help; I didn't even think about it when I was thrown into doing my very first drag performance. My close friend called to say, "You know how you have talked about doing drag, but you keep talking yourself out of it. Well, tonight is your night. We need you because the other people backed out that we booked for the show." They laughed. I freaked out for a few minutes. In my head I screamed, "I don't have anything I need!" They said, "Calm down we got you." I have stage fright bad, so that made me freak out more. Once I got in drag, I didn't have that problem. I learned later on that my drag performances kind of helped me work through some things, but didn't always help me with my depression. I would find myself trying to drink it away by get drunk every time I was at the bar which was wrong! It has taken a ton of work. I am proud to say that I can go to a bar and do drag and not drink any alcohol! I might have a couple of drinks a year now. Drag can help some. Keep in mind, it is ok to ask for help from the people close to you that do drag also.

❀ It's really difficult for me to remember every thought I had when I started drag. I don't think I directly thought that it would impact my mental health, but I do remember feeling joy and excitement around the new possibility of becoming a drag queen. At the time I was super cis out of drag and had never played with my Gender Expression, outside of painting my nails. It was like I went into a new world of possibilities I had never previously explored. It was very exciting. I can't remember every detail.

❀ Nope. I had no idea that I would love being in men's clothes and performing as my true self. I stopped wearing women's clothing altogether. I enjoy it at home too.

❀ I honestly didn't think drag would help me at all before I started doing it. I was tired of being depressed and bullied all the time. I thought that maybe it could help lift my spirits and maybe some other young people could see me doing it.

❀ I didn't find drag, it found me. It wasn't in a depressive stage in my life, quite the opposite. I associate much of my drag persona with a very happy time in my life when I was just starting out and had a great support system who helped me become the traveling entertainer that I am today!

❀ I had no idea how much performing drag would help me when I first started. It was when I started choosing songs that meant something to me that I started noticing the change within myself. All of the emotions I had been keeping buried inside myself were brought to the surface, and I was able to allow them to flow out of me through the music. The lyrics helped me to say what I had always needed to say but never had the words for. It let me connect with people in the audience as well as other entertainers who were able to recognize what I was going through. I was finally able to start healing.

❀ I don't know if I thought it would help me with my depression, but I thought it would help me with my gender expression and identity before I knew what my gender identity was.

❀ The positive effect drag has on my mental health is a unexpected benefit. I credit this to the fact that drag helped me answer many questions about myself about my gender and sexuality and built my confidence. This ultimately helped me begin to feel more "myself." Drag allowed me to express myself and that lessened some of my depression. Hiding who you are is a heavy feeling that pulls you away from joy. Drag helped me find my way towards joy and light in a way I could never have previously imagined.

❀ I honestly never thought about it helping me before I started doing drag. After a few months I was able to pick out songs that expressed my feelings and allowed me to release some of those emotions.

❀ I didn't have depression when I first started doing drag.

❀ Drag paved the way to self-discovery. It allowed me to "test the waters" as the male I had always known myself to be, but no one else up to that point could not see. I had no idea when I began that it would shape the rest of my life in a way I'd only thought possible in my thoughts.

❀ I always knew that there were "things" out there to help with my depression that I hadn't discovered yet. DRAG just happens to be one of those things so far.

❀ I really didn't realize how happy drag would make me or how wonderful it would be. All of my drag is for charity. My drag is my way if giving back.

❀ No, I thought it was just something to distract me.

❀ No. I thought I would do this for a few years, but here I am with thirty years later. At first, I think it was about trying to fit in and exploring myself.

❀ I never thought drag would help my depression. I never put those two things together. However now I can see how wonderful a distraction it could be, to sit there and paint your face for a couple hours. I can bring so much joy, laughter and happiness to other people. I didn't start doing drag to help with my depression. I started because I wanted to put my own stamp on the industry. Drag is a fantastic outlet on so many fronts and can help the battle with depression.

❀ Never in my wildest dreams would I imagine that something involving makeup would help me. I am so glad that I dipped into it and found this outlet. Drag has helped me so much!

❀ I never thought I would put myself on stage to perform for others. I've always had anxiety and been self-conscious. Never wanted to be the center of attention growing up. When I found out about drag, I was enthralled with it. It has given me so much joy and happiness.

❀ I only realized drag served an antidepressant role in my life after nearly a year of doing drag. Interestingly, it was only in applying makeup to my face and creating a character that I found my most authentic self.

❀ I knew drag would help me immensely. I embrace drag every day and live in such a way the area sees me who I truly am. There are moments many are afraid of it. Though adrenaline gets me through glittery and lighter situations.

❀ I honestly didn't think Drag would help me as much as it did with my depression. I went from not wanting to leave the house to constantly performing because it made me happy. My mood swings got far in between and I'm happier most of the time now.

❀ I started doing drag being part of a shadow cast for Rocky Horror Picture Show. It helped build up my self-esteem to feel more comfortable being around people that would talk to me face to face rather than say bad things about me behind my back.

❀ Honestly, I didn't think that drag would help at all! When I started, it just seemed like a way to express myself that I couldn't do when I was younger. My dad is a Baptist pastor. When I performed for the first time, the audience was cheering me on and loving it; it felt amazing. This was something that I've always been too scared to do for fear of judgement. I saw the effect it had on people. I realized that I had so much power in myself to do what I've always wanted to do: entertain, educate, inspire, and provoke thought through an art form that I'm passionate about. My biggest worry was that I would never get to do that in life. After seeing that I literally did it, I went backstage and started crying from happiness for the first time in years.

Chapter Four, Question Four
"How do you handle preparing to do
DRAG when you feel depressed?"

❀ It is almost impossible to get ready when you are depressed. Sitting there staring in your eyes, knowing the secrets within. It is a fight. I want to cancel. Every bone in my body is telling me to go home. I know once I go on stage, I will feel better. I concentrate. I say to myself, "Get out of your head." Sometimes I listen to music on my headset. If I am really depressed, I won't talk to the other entertainers. I want them to go away and leave me alone. I focus on my makeup… Oh those eyes. I think about my performance, the audience, my persona and knowing for a moment I can escape. I want to escape. Getting ready helps me prepare for that rescue.

❀ It's hard to handle at first but I sit and stare at my makeup, take deep breaths, pick up a glue stick, and start putting on my makeup. I play some calming music and my worries starts to fade while I'm putting my face on. As I get ready it feels like my mood completely changes and the depression melts away. I have nothing to worry about in that moment.

❀ I try to put myself in the mindset of my drag "persona" and attempt to push my problems to the back of my mind. I'm a different person on stage and much of my worries disappear when I'm actually performing.

❀ When I am depressed, I actually love getting ready. The process distracts me and allows me for a few minutes to forget the pain of my depression.

❀ Prep for show includes my clothing and music. I have certain people I've appointed drag coordinators before the show. My brain jumps into drag mode. It anticipates the good feeling I'm will get from doing drag. I go, go, go… so I'll end up being prepared for a show hours earlier than needed.

❀ I have trained myself to get angry with my depression when preparing for a show. It pushes me to work even harder on costumes. Problem is my obsessive-compulsive disorder (OCD) will kick in and it won't let me mess up costumes. Once I am on stage, getting into character is enhanced. When the show is over, I have a period of letdown. I often feel like I could have done much better. With that comes a sort of mourning. A period of grieving. A good cry can help. It's hard on facebook because usually the people who were in the show, want to talk the next day and I just really do not want to connect with people after the show. Once I have come back around, it is like my thought process in enhanced and ideas begin to flood in for the next show. The circle of entertainment begins again. I have found one thing that does absolutely help me deal with this is my kids and husband. Always encouraging me and loving me unconditionally.

❀ It's really difficult when I'm depressed. I usually spend much of my time listening to upbeat music and pick numbers that would take some dancing, or that are campy/comedy. I also watch lots of funny movies and shows. My therapist calls it immersive therapy, and it definitely helps to have something that pushes you into those better thoughts and feelings. Especially when you have to act it out for others.

❀ I push through it, because I know the final outcome of the hair, outfit and the whole look will make me feel better.

❀ It's hard to handle but I will sit in front of my makeup countering energy to do something. I feel a tad bit better when I start painting my face. Once my costume is on, I feel like I have beat depression back another day.

❀ It's not easy. Sometimes it can even become overwhelming to get ready while depressed. I make sure I have plenty of time to get ready just in case I'm struggling before the show. Having more time relieves some of my anxiety and prevents unnecessary pressures. I also listen to my favorite music or watch some of my favorite previous performances to try to inspire myself to get together. Once I begin, I often feel better after I finish and see myself in drag!

❀ When I'm depressed I honest don't want to perform. I do it begrudgingly. I'm one of those people that when they promise to do something they do it, so I show up. The funny thing is once I sit at that makeup mirror, my mood slowly starts to change. I'm no longer myself with problems. I'm the entertainer, the old party girl that will do anything to make people laugh. Also, the girls I work with are the best. Their love and support help me. They always make me feel loved.

❀ I give myself more time to do something unusual with it. Try a different style of makeup or add something to my costume, something experimental helps me feel like it's new and interesting again.

❀ I would say I don't always handle preparing for Drag well when depressed. I usually leave things to the last minute to get the anxiety energy to be able to do the things I need to do. One of the steps I take to try and avoid this though is to work with others. I try to find people to keep me company or collaborate with. I find I can more easily create and prepare without having to activate the anxiety energy. It is not always possible and I end up falling back onto the anxiety energy. I have never been in a position where I needed to cancel or back out. I can always get it done in the end. Honestly 90% of the time I feel better after performing and being with people at the shows or events. Another trick? I make sure to have simple routines and costumes for depression/low energy times. In those instances, I focus on connecting performances to how I am feeling. I think some people have this view that all drag performances need to be flashy and exciting. Yet some of my best feedback and connection with the audience comes from my lower key, soul-searching performances. I think it is because they are connecting with peoples' souls and lived experiences a bit more.

❀ I give myself permission to do a song about how I am feeling. I spend my drives to work finding just the right one. Then I offset that one with a song that has a way to release positive energy. I give myself two hours on show day to get into my drag persona's personality. The transformation comes together as I am playing my songs and picking out my outfits and accessories. I can trust as an entertainer that I will be professional, no matter what I am feeling. Drag is an amazing outlet for me.

❀ To be honest, my depression can sometimes force me to cancel an appearance. This can cause a deeper depression. It is usually cured by the next performance where I am able to pour all my pent-up emotion.

❀ I feel like I handle them fairly well when I prepare to do DRAG. I'm very fortunate to have an amazing partner, who is very patient and understanding of me and my mental struggles. If I'm starting to feel the creeping dread, I'll ask her to hold me and give me a "soul-crushing hug" because the deep pressure helps to soothe my negative thoughts and regulate my emotions. I also go into the bathroom, stare at my reflection in the mirror, and repeat my mantra: "I am smart, I am kind, I am important, and I am damn good looking."

❀ Drag for me is a form of anti-depression. When I get depressed, I will paint how I am feeling. I pick my numbers for shows based on my mood. Now managing depression and bi polar while in pageant mode is entirely different. I've gone into some pageants as the favored winner and/or first alternate but finished dead last because the bi-polar express took over and sends me crashing. I will not do another pageant until my bi-polar is 100%

in check because that crash was a waste of my team's time to have me ready. Depression and bi-polar are two separate beasts and need treated separately. Drag is one of my anti depression "drugs."

🎭 I have to push myself to get in drag when my depression is at its worse even if it's just for fun or practicing my makeup skills. I know anytime I am in drag, I feel different, better. I am able to be someone else for a while and it helps.

🎭 I handle each situation differently, with love and care, all of which depends greatly on the specific circumstances. Sometimes this leads me to having to make the difficult, yet rare decision to drop out of a show and other-times, persevering through the internal struggle thus using performance as an emotional outlet. Self-care should always come first though, you will not be able to give the audience or yourself your all, if you're at your worst. In my experience, I realized the majority of times when I had pushed through the agony of getting out of bed and made it to the stage during a depressive episode, just being in that supportive, uplifting environment significantly helped pull me out of those depressive ruts. I often listen to upbeat music while show prepping to help alter my mood as well! Drag also gives me a platform to channel those powerful emotions into my performances and provides a refreshing environment for me to step away from the four walls of my bedroom. Lastly, many of my recent acts are commentary on the current political climate which has helped me process the anti-LGBTQ+ legislation & overturning of Roe v Wade.

🎭 When I'm feelings depressed and overwhelmed, I just think about how I'm going to make someone smile and have fun by coming to see the show.

🎭 I have to give myself lots of time to paint, prepare, have a breakdown, cry, ruin my face and start all over again. Slowly, I start to feel my drag character waking up inside of me as the look starts to come together; he's power, confidence, comedy, vitality and sexuality, all the things that I struggle to hold on to in depression.

🎭 I always get ready at home, alone. It's a stressful day leading up to the time I begin to paint my face. Anxiety is high. I make sure things are packed and/or laid out for me to get dressed when ready. I sit at my makeup table and organize everything I intend to use. My OCD comes in handy here. This time preparing and the process itself are quite calming and really aid in the transformation. As I start to paint and see the beginnings of the look I planned, the mental switch from "me" to "her" begins. It honestly takes me about four hours from the first touch of foundation to a finished face. That time is used to build myself up and allow the outgoing personality of my character to emerge. I'm never fully confident once I'm ready to leave, but the showgirl in me kicks in and the show must go on! I always approach this is an actor playing a role and my primary function is to be entertaining. Regardless of how I feel inside, I cannot disappoint the people that have to see me.

❀ I make sure I choose music that either brings me joy or songs that express what I am currently feeling. I also allow myself much more time to do my makeup and get ready so I don't feel rushed if I'm slowly moving.

❀ Preparing for a drag show when I'm depressed can be hard. Especially when trying to choose the right songs to entertain the audience. You don't want to pull them into depression with you. I have learned to turn to my fellow performers for inspiration and motivation to help me prepare. Music is a great healing tool if you do it right. Getting into drag and performing your songs can really help you release those emotions and thoughts and be able to tell a story of happier things. I allow myself the room to heal through it the best I can.

❀ If I'm fighting depression that day then before I perform, I hit a hundred balls at the batting cage until I'm too tired to think about anything but inflicting severe pain on the Taliban. Anger can be an unhappy person's best friend and be a fantastic motivator.

❀ I blare dorky '80's music over my surround sound system. It gets me in a better mood every time.

❀ If I'm feeling anxious or depressed before a show it doesn't clear until I finish my first number. Seeing how happy the audience is to watch me perform, gets me back into a correct state of mind. When I'm getting ready during those moments of doubt, I remind myself that what I'm about to do is not only going to help me but so many other people who may be struggling with the same thoughts or issues. It's a glorious thing to know you made someone's day better just by being yourself and that they came to support your art.

❀ When my depression sets, there are times that I don't want to do anything at all and that includes doing drag. Even though I don't want to do anything when feeling depressed, I recognize that I can't just sit around and do nothing because I'm just going to feel even more depressed. I make myself do things. When I do drag, I am in my happy place. It's like I was never depressed because of the energy I receive from the crowd and fellow performers.

❀ When I'm depressed and aware of it, I make a plan for the day. I'll start by giving myself an extra two hours that day, if possible, because I know my mania spikes while getting ready. I try to lay out everything that I am going to need ahead of time so I'm not frantically searching for it. I then put on a Native American flute music station on Pandora and smoke copious amounts of marijuana before and while getting ready!

❀ When I'm depressed before a show, I listen to my music selections, give myself plenty of extra time. I'm a perfectionist when it comes to drag. I try to keep my mind occupied and focus only on that night's performance. I write a list of what to wear and what to pack so I make sure I have everything I need for the show. I don't drink any alcoholic beverages until I've reached my destination as it can cause me to be distracted by depressing thoughts. Once I'm at the club and on stage to welcome to audience, I feel so much better.

❀ If I'm in a depression and have a show or booking, the only way I can snap out of it is through music. One of my mentors who is no longer with us used to tell me, "To look pretty you have to paint pretty, and to paint pretty you have to listen to pretty painting music." It used to baffle me and make me laugh hysterically, but it's something I do even now. I have to listen to music that is fun and uplifting and powerful. Songs by Joan Jett, Pat Benatar, Bonnie Tyler, Katy Perry, Madonna, Cher, and all the greats. Within a few minutes it's almost like I am an entirely different person.

❀ I'm too hard on myself as a King in a Queen's world. I feel the need to work extra hard. On my worst days everyone is telling me to just reuse numbers or not stress about a show. I feel like I've let everyone down by not making a new outfit and new mix. It only makes the depression worse, because my inner voice is telling me ten times louder, "I'm not good enough and I should just quit." Thankfully, I also suffer from severe ADHD and am a whiz at throwing things together last minute. I'll spend days laying on the couch telling myself to just give up and then bang out a new outfit the night before in a matter of hours.

❀ I start with the parts of planning my show that are the easiest and most creative. It is a struggle, but the end result is worth it.

❀ When I make an obligation to something, I am there rain, sleet, snow (blizzard), sore, and tired. The only thing that keeps me from going is being sick. It may take me all day to get my stuff packed, outfits and songs picked because I keep changing my mind. I have to tell myself all day that this will help give me a push out of my funk. I get to see my friends that hang out with the people that come to see us perform and make to them smile. I like seeing them having a good time which helps get me back on track. Some days were very hard to get out of bed to start my day and I would be grumpy. I didn't want to go but I went anyway.

❀ I think of the songs I'm doing and the meaning I'm portraying for the night. I remember and think about plans for tomorrow. Always think of tomorrow and you know it can be different.

❀ Thinking of it from a professional standpoint, my brain usually has no problem with clicking over to work mode. Once I hit that stage, I'm usually fine. It's that brief high, those slim minutes of getaway, and then once I'm off it slowly creeps back in. There have been a few times where I really was not feeling it whatsoever, and it definitely can show up in my makeup, socialization, and performance. I tell myself, "My makeup can be simple that day." If I fuck up my performance, it happens to everyone. Sometimes you just have to accept that you cannot be at 100% all the time, and that's okay. It's not necessarily healthy, but I try to have a drink before I go on stage too if I'm not feeling on my "A" game. Moderation is key, and not being dependent on it. Know yourself and your limits.

❀ Same way as any other performances. Rest, sleep good then go do my drag job.

❀ If I'm in my feelings and not feeling my normal self, socialization with my fellow performers and the people that go to support me will help uplift me. I'm overly self-critical as I get ready. I normally spend the first moments staring myself down, take a deep breath and take what the doctor gave me. I always feel better once I start painting my face, to show the confidence that everyone sees when I step on stage. The smiles from others reacting to my art seems to part the clouds.

❀ For me being in drag lets me be someone I am not and maybe someone that people will like more than me. I don't always like me and I know most people who know me out of drag don't like me either. I get to change who I am on the outside. It allows me as a performer to be somebody else that people may like, so it makes me less depressed about real life.

❀ Preparing for drag, contributing my time or efforts actually helps pull me out of depression. It provides me with something I love to focus on.

❀ I actually get excited about the joy I bring to the audience. It makes me focus on my character and music.

❀ Getting ready to perform when I am feeling depressed is by far one of the hardest things for me to do. I have however figured out that by sitting down, throwing on some music that counters my mood, and grabbing some colors that match my mood helps. I make sure to prime my face, massaging each muscle as I go which relaxes me and gets me in the mood. Finally, I let my brain switch over to full drag character, which in my case is very different than my normal daily self, successfully allowing the stress of daily life and depression to melt away.

❀ When I'm depressed and have a show, getting my costumes and songs together helps my depression. The music I chose definitely reflects what mood and state I am in.

❀ It takes some oomph to get started or motivated, but usually the makeup stage of preparing helps to clear my head more than I would have thought. The hard part is getting out of the blanket-fort to start.

❀ If I'm feeling down and depressed, I just start to think of my songs I will be performing that night or how the energy from the audience will make me feel. As I start applying my makeup, I instantly forget how I was feeling and immediately get into a better mood. Drag is my happy place!

❀ If I'm feeling really depressed before a gig, I turn on some music and blare out all my thoughts or take a ride to my favorite getaway place while listening to music clearing my head. So far, I haven't had to cancel a gig due to my depression, I normally just tough it through.

❀ I focus on inspiration from other people's drag. I see their beauty and it reminds me I'm not alone.

❀ I do I choose uplifting songs from the '70s and early '80s along with makeup and wardrobe for at least four numbers. I arrive at the venue I have been booked reflecting my options. I try to relive my childhood by paying tribute to the Divas of that period in time and the fans reaction is truly a blessing that heals my depression.

❀ This is a tough one. Sticking to a routine helps me, even if I don't feel like doing it. Depending on the severity of my depression flare, sometimes I'll just focus entirely on getting myself ready and don't spend much time chatting with the other entertainers. Other times I'll let them know that I'm feeling a bit off that night and then take a few extra minutes to get myself into "the zone." If there's a specific issue in my life that my brain has latched onto, then I might talk to one of the other entertainers about it.

❀ It depends on how bad is the depression and my physical health. If it's a gig I've committed to in advance, I try and remember, "I'm getting paid and they usually are positive experiences." It's an opportunity to express myself and hopefully be around people that support me.

❀ When I am depressed, I have to force myself the day of the show because it is hard for me to want to do it and I don't feel putting my emotions out there will help. The hint I have found is that it really does help. It also allows me not to just set at home to wallow in my depressed state of mind.

❀ Sometimes I get so depressed that the music changes a thousand of times before my show. Performing saves me from dwelling in my own head. Music speaks volumes and in every language.

❀ I usually end up going through the motions. I've had to back out of a show during a time where I was under extreme depression and stress. While it hurt and felt embarrassing to back out, it was a reminder to myself that if I don't figure out a way to stabilize myself, I wouldn't be able to do anything, including drag. Drag motivates me to heal. I've had to acknowledge to myself that my health has to come first, and knowing that drag was waiting for me when I was feeling better helped me push forward.

❀ I usually end up going through the motions. I've had to back out of a show during a time where I was under extreme depression and stress. It hurt and felt embarrassing to back out, but it was a reminder to myself that if I don't figure out a way to stabilize myself, I wouldn't be able to do anything, including drag. Drag motivates me to heal. I've had to acknowledge to myself that my health has to come first, and knowing that drag was waiting for me when I was feeling better helped me push forward.

❀ I look myself in the mirror before my make up and play the song "I Say a Little Prayer" by Aretha Franklin and think about my feminine side. She can do and be anything I want to be. It's an escape from reality.

❀ It's difficult to ramp up your energy when you're depressed and prepping for a show. I usually put on a movie or music I really like to watch.

❀ It's often when I find myself at low points that throw myself head first into my craft. It is during those moments that I examine the circumstances weighing on me and pulling me down that I immerse myself in music until I find that song which seems to capture my experience in a way traditional speech falls short of being able to convey. I am able to put internal emotions into an external context that others can not only understand, but relate to themselves... even if the message is a heavy one.

❀ I listen to music as I get ready which helps clear my mind. It helps me get ready to perform mentally and calms me.

❀ I surround myself with others who give me positive reinforcement or I listen to music. I'm a no drama kind of King.

❀ There are days that I just don't want to do anything. I will do my makeup and think to myself, "You look horrible." Once I am performing or around others, who say "You look amazing," all dread and self-doubt melt away.

❀ In all honesty I didn't think it would help in the beginning. I've done drag over twenty years and looking back I only made it a creative way to express my feminine side.

❀ Music. I feel the energy by popping my headphones in and just letting the music take me.

❀ Music really helps me focus. I get lost in the music. I always visualize my numbers in my head as practice; I play the music and just think about what I want to do for the show as a distraction.

❀ The very process of preparing to do drag is enough to bring me out of depression. It is better than selective serotonin reuptake inhibitors (SSRIs) and a therapy session combined.

❀ When I visualize on the event or on the day the Queen comes out and turns the depression right around. I think I give myself a hug and kiss and say its ok. It's ok not to be okay in an overwhelming situation.

❀ Getting into face and into my outfit really helps me get out of a depressing state. There are days when I'll be depressed but as soon as I put on the music that I listen to, it inspires my makeup and my mood uplifts. I'm able to pull myself out of the depression and into my drag persona!

❀ Depression can hit in waves. I cannot always catch or recognize a trigger. There have been many occasions where my depression makes me feel like I wanted to cancel. I would not feel like getting dressed or being around people. I would have my phone in my hand ready to send a cancellation message but I stopped myself. I forced myself to press through because I knew I'd benefit from release that drag gives. Depression is no joke but drag helps.

❀ I say to myself when I am preparing to go to a club, "I am going to make this crowd happy that they came out and saw me perform tonight."

Chapter Five, Question Five
"What does DRAG do for you to deal with
your depression when you are not on stage?"

❀ When I need it to distract me from reality, I go out to other shows. The energy and fun of it usually helps cheer me up.

❀ The week before the show it gives me lots of busy work to keep my mind off of things. I'm making costumes and styling wigs instead of worrying about gloom and doom. When I'm in the dressing room I have my sisters to cheer me up and give me support. There is no cure though like being on that stage.

❀ In drag, I am totally different person. It helps take the reality of me as a boy and turns it around to a happy proud woman. Happy being the key word there.

❀ It gives me something to look back on and raise the thoughts of "if I can create these things that bring entertainment and joy to this many people even in the middle of my worst moments then I can make it through this too."

❀ I am at my happiest when I am designing my costumes which I spend countless hours on. When I begin to feel an anxiety attack coming on, I get all my materials out and work, work, work! Now that my kids are all grown. I have way too much time on my hands, so I work just like at a regular job building the most complicated costumes. In these later years, my hubby and I have become so comfortable with each other that we spend little time talking or being intimate. Since he began to trans to female, it's like were just roommates and that is adding to my depression. It is actually more like grieving. So now all I have is my drag to keep me company. I have actually begun to write a book about my life story. Though I doubt I will ever finish it. Drag is my medication for depression and anxiety. Whether I am watching thousands of music videos, looking up the latest fashions, sewing, gluing, and mapping out material, the rest of my time is watching every RuPaul episode to get inspiration! I am terrified what my life will be when I am no longer able to do drag.

❀ Drag helps my body image and self-image. It can make me feel so happy after a show, no matter how the day previously went.

❀ Drag always gives me something to work on. A good performance idea can stop me from entering a depressive spiral. I can get myself motivated by making props, mixing songs, or going out to thrift shops. Drag doesn't completely eliminate depression, but it does soothe the worst parts of depression.

❀ Being on stage and performing are a release for me. I almost always do songs that speak to me and my life in that moment. It gives me purpose and hope in times I may be very lacking in it. It is when I feel the most alive and worthy.

❀ When I start feeling depressed, I start making new drag outfits I have a creative mind that allows me to focus on things that make me happy.

❀ Practicing makeup, making new costume pieces and learning new skills to incorporate into my drag is always helpful when I'm not performing, and for my depression. It gives me something to do and something to look forward to doing.

❀ The planning and creation process allows me to escape some feelings. It allows me to work with creativity, to be a distraction and try to get out of the funk.

❀ I would say more so my Drag family helps me deal with depression when not on stage. People who I did not know a few years ago have become my sounding board, my cheering section, my family. Keeping busy between shows helps some with my depression, the prep work and excitement. But, the family dinners, the random "just checking in" text messages, and even the silly memes or TikToks we send throughout the day or week... that is what means the most.

❀ It definitely gives you a great distraction. You can also pull inspiration for performances from your depression. I've used things that led me to be further depressed to create concepts for various routines and mixes. Hearing the audiences react to them makes it worth it and helps defeat the depression.

❀ It gives me an outlet, being able to be creative whether it is costumes, hair, different ways to apply makeup, seeking out song choices, et cetera. Everything leading up to being on stage allows my mind to keep active and hold my attention to keep me busy. This gives me something to look forward to doing.

❀ Drag gives me something to focus on and to work towards. In addition to depression, I also have ADHD, so having a channel for the hyperactivity brings the depression along. I know I can't sit around and be sad, so I have a specific thing I can be proud of myself for completing, which helps me complete other tasks.

❀ It's a better way for my mind to wonder from intrusive thoughts. Whether it be focusing on a show I have coming up in the future and the outfits and all the accessories. It's a distraction thinking of all the little things that will get a rise out of an audience and bring a smile to my face. I have more friends and chosen family because of drag. I have that support system to help uplift me outside of my drag circle. This gives me a distraction for more upcoming events to keep my mind going and not overthinking.

❀ Stoning and creating outfits are very relaxing for me. I can shut off my mind and just be creative. I am nearing the end of my drag career. I can't see myself ever stopping with creating drag wear. I have been held back due to time constraints and money. Once I am no longer on stage, I can see myself continuing and expanding that part of drag as long as I can.

❀ It definitely gives me a distraction from everything in my life. If I can be creative in my mind, I won't have time to worry about every little thing that I cannot control. Even when I am sitting in my room, I can feel a little better.

❀ When I'm not on stage and depression occurs, I like to watch old videos of pageants from all the systems out there. I have so many beautiful friends and sisters on those tapes. It helps me to cry the depression away. I revel in my forty-year history of doing DRAG. It warms my heart to go through my enormous scrap book of pictures from the past. Being retired from DRAG, sometimes that's all I've got to reflect on. My sisters are my therapy when I'm feeling low.

❀ When my depression sneaks up on me while I am not onstage, I quickly turn to my saved music albums and begin work on what I want to do in next performance. I begin to work on costuming and concepts. When I can't work on any other those things, I turn to my drag family and my biological family for support. They help keep me grounded and help me rediscover my path.

❀ Drag serves me when I'm not on stage because each act takes lots of committed rehearsal, creative passion and innovation. This creative journey is always rewarding in itself because it helps me emotionally process trauma when I'm devising concepts for each act to send meaningful messages to the audience. The artistic process is also an empowering self-journey of bringing your imagination to life while also serving as a healing approach. The acts I create are almost always a response to something I'm currently struggling with or enthusiastic about in my life. When I'm not on the stage I also learn to DIY (Do it Yourself) many costuming techniques such as rhinestoning patterns, applying spikes & patches to bedazzle jackets, and even creating bad ass tearaway pants. Over the past four years I've realized that learning how to personalize my costume pieces not only distracts me from my depression but also allows me to be innovative and creative in different ways so its fulfilling in its own unique form. I also recognized that when I'm off the stage, drag has helped me explore my gender identity and expression which has significantly boosted my self-confidence to help express myself more authentically.

❀ When not on stage I'm like an old crow… looking at all my sparklies. That's cataloging my jewelry. They do cheer me up!

❀ Drag has so many benefits in my life. I use my drag persona, not only to entertain but also, now, as an outreach to those in our community.

Whenever I feel down or just not myself, I first remember the "job" I have dedicated myself to do that hopefully and prayerfully will reach someone and help them in some way. I work on new songs, new hair, and new ideas. Most importantly, I am collaborating my thoughts and ideas for a possible one woman show about my life. The moment you allow depression to overtake you and your creativity, the harder it is to regain. If it goes so far as to cause you to cancel show after show and just not be yourself, as it did to me in the fall of 2021, then the recovery and trust with others is almost like starting over.

❀ Drag gives me something to smile about. My main goal as a drag artist is to make others smile and for them to forget about their own problems. When I perform, I let my mind mostly forget about my life off stage and focus on my performance.

❀ The only help there is for depression are medications and therapy. Drag is my happy place because I can be who I truly am in life. No more faking that I am a chick. It helps. Kings don't offer any fellowship unless it's a working cast at a club that offers nightly drag shows. There are none close to me, so I don't become jaded. I don't do drag locally. I get moments of pleasure on stage because I was trained classically. I did music from age of three, conservatory training at Julliard, 392 live performances, a third of them in Drag, drama and choreography. Even in the metal band we used choreography.

❀ When I need to stone an outfit or make something, it actually makes my depression worse off stage, minus a distraction here and there. The toxicity in the community here is horrible and as a King trying to make it in a Queen's world, I tend to over exert myself trying to succeed or take everything personally causing my depression to spiral even more out of control.

❀ When I am actually on stage, it is a chance to leave "me" behind and become the character of the song I'm doing. I can disconnect from the struggles of real life, even if only for a few hours. Drag doesn't help me, personally, when I'm not on stage. Not being on stage highlights how alone, unloved, invisible and unimportant I think I am. I know that statement is not entirely true, but that is what's in my head much of the time. I work through that every day.

❀ Drag doesn't do anything for me when I am not on stage. If I am not on stage then I am not performing, so I have to deal with every day real life struggles.

❀ Choosing music to prepare for a show has always been the go-to when I'm not on stage. I will put the headphones on, listen to a song and visualize performing it. From the costume, to the lyrics to envisioning how I will interact with the audience based on the song.

❀ I pick music to lift my spirits. The whole thing is really an escape from the feeling that I am going through. Knowing later, I will look out at the smiling and dancing audience and they will bring me joy.

❀ The ability to transform and create the illusion of my stage persona has always been a stress release. Getting lost in the moment keep depression at bay.

❀ Listening to all the songs I'm getting ready to perform, styling outfits, hair and practicing makeup just makes me come out of the funk when it hits me.

❀ Drag actually isn't all on a stage. I've figured out that my character is powerful even without a stage, that he has a platform that he can use to create a better world. When I am not on stage and feeling depressed, sometimes I'll actually practice some makeup for an upcoming show, or practice nailing every lyric in the song. Other times however, I'll put myself in full drag and use the platforms I have to talk about world issues. Talking about world issues and issues in my life as my drag character, instead of myself, allows me to open up a bit more and talk through what is bothering me.

❀ Taking the time to get my songs ready and my drag outfits forces me to get out of my head. The thoughts that when I do perform, my drag family will be there for hugs and support. I do not even have to say how I am feeling. They give hugs and positive energy to me. Without even knowing I'm having a really crazy day. It gives me that thought, just one more day, and I will be with my family.

❀ When I am in my head, I like to go through pictures from previous shows but more importantly from Prides' past. When I am doubting myself or feeling that I am not making an impact I will look at those photos and reflect on how I was feeling at that exact moment and it makes me smile. If I get deep in my thoughts, I will bring those feelings to life with some makeup and share my creations on social media. I hide my feelings and thoughts very well. Bringing them to life with living room drag allows me to be vulnerable and find a bit of inner peace.

❀ Preparing for a show keeps me busy and brings me up. Everything from shopping for new outfits, selecting my music, rehearsing my numbers, styling my wigs, and practicing makeup all immediately put me in a good mood!

❀ Drag keeps me busy off stage. I'm always looking for new ways to perform on stage with the right music. Currently I'm working on rebranding my image, so I am searching lots of different styles.

❀ It gives me a superhero alter ego and she's super powerful. Knowing she exists keeps me going day to day.

❀ Buying the things needed to do the show helps take my mind elsewhere. Can be anywhere.

❀ When I am not on stage, I usually try to keep depression at bay by staying creative. It takes time spent not on stage to come up with the music, choreography, costume ideas, sewing, practicing, et cetera. I realize that my depression has returned when I'm not making art. When I find myself not expressing creatively for quite a while, I need to start my self-care routine to try and pull myself back out of the darkness. Sometimes when I'm feeling real down, even just small motivational things can help, such as watching a show where the costumes inspire me. I still would point that back to drag helping me feel my most genuine.

❀ Drag has given me an entirely new family, one that's even larger than my extended biological family. I know that my drag family is always there for me no matter what. My character personality is also always there for me. I can bring my drag persona forward whenever I need a little extra help being strong enough to handle a situation. I find it's easier to reach out to people and ask for help if I'm in that character mindset, and I can be more honest about how I'm really feeling instead of brushing it all off as nothing.

❀ I find my time not on stage is when DRAG helps me the most with my depression. It gets me out of my normal daily work and life routine. It engages my creative side as I have to find a song or songs, edit them and come up with the routines, make-up and costumes. I will sometimes add videos that I make. These creative processes bring me much joy. It gives me a chance to reach out and engage with people in a fun way that lasts longer than the time I spend on the stage.

❀ DRAG helps me to redirect my emotions and focus my energy on doing something productive when I am not on stage. In my DRAG experience, I put a lot of thought and planning into my upcoming performance gigs which includes my song choices, costuming, and choreography. I always try to make sure that I look and perform at my best level; I can't afford to let my current mental state affect my stagecraft and reputation.

❀ I have something to focus on when I am not on stage. I can focus my thoughts and energy to planning what I want to do next. Like how I will express the message in the song I picked, by focusing on dance moves, the clothes I choose and even the accessories that I bring out.

❀ Filling my mind with imagination and hope. I can turn what I am facing in my life into performances to help me. Purpose is a powerful tool for depression. Just knowing I can perform is step one for me. Figuring out how I help my fans as well as myself is step two. It moves me forward with purpose.

❀ DRAG helps me to redirect my emotions and focus my energy on doing something productive when I am not on stage. In my DRAG experience, I put a lot of thought and planning into my upcoming performance gigs which includes my song choices, costuming, and choreography. I always try to make sure that I look and perform at my best level; I can't afford to let my current mental state affect my stagecraft and reputation.

❀ Drag helps me to focus my energy on doing something I love and bring the emotion to the stage. I always try to make sure that I perform the best I can. Off stage, drag makes me work on putting my energy into the creative side like stoning, music choice and outfits. Keeps my mind focus on the goal and out of the head space.

❀ Drag has given me a community of support. People to talk to about what's going on in my life. Drag gives me something to look forward to - bringing my art and story. My vulnerability is appreciated. I've also recently got into stoning and trying to better my costuming which gives me stuff to focus on, and I feel like I'm making progress and being productive. The cool thing about drag is there also isn't a deadline, which helps and I can re-frame it as a hobby.

❀ It's a creative outlet for me. All the designing and making it really helps. Also diving deep into music lets me lose myself, especially when I'm in a bad place.

❀ I found drag after a rape. Drag saved me. I was able to leave my home, I was able to live a life I thought I was going to end. No one was able to get through to me, I felt alone, dirty, unworthy of love or friendship. I was scared I was pregnant, that I was HIV positive, I was waiting for the next shoe to fall. Putting on a face, clothes and a persona I myself am not, have me power... power over fear, my own mind and over my situation. I'm thankful every day.

❀ Preparing for a show, event, or pageant is exciting because I can focus on what the audience or judges will think, say, and feel when I perform for them. It makes me feel good.

❀ Not much to be honest. It keeps me out of trouble and busy making costumes or learning new numbers.

❀ Prepping for a show is a full-time job on its own, there is music, theme, choreography and costumes to work on. I enjoy getting a new idea and putting it into action.

❀ Drag, with all its elements, is never confined solely to the stage for me. This, in large part, is due to my building my performances on aspects of my own life and experiences, rather than Drag being an escape or distraction from the effects of my depression. Drag is my way of processing feelings and emotions that would otherwise lock inside until they consumed me entirely.

❀ The confidence I found on the stage spread into my everyday life. Drag changed me even off stage for the good. I believed in myself again. I was comfortable with myself. I could live once again inside of my own skin.

❀ When not on stage my drag keeps my mind moving and open. I think about what I can do for future performances or how I may be able to help others with ideas for their next stage performance.

❀ Drag let's my imagination run being creative by designing my next outfit or planning my next look. I think of my next song and who I am looking forward to who I will perform with on stage.

❀ When not on stage I find doing photo shoots and TikTok videos bring my mood up. Drag is my happy place.

❀ It makes me feel genuinely happy. I don't necessarily feel happy on most of my everyday life. I mostly sit in a state of apathy and almost play a part to the people in my life. Drag makes me feel like I can be myself and I can be creative and it's ok. It makes me happy to perform.

❀ Drag reminds me of my worth, my value, and my true beauty.

❀ Drag is every day. Drag is life. I let the persona become the real way for me. Underneath the skin, there are many scars. Though on top of it, reality gets to see the true side of who I am. I embrace my Queen every day.

❀ Drag can be an outlet for me to relieve my depression. Especially if the audience is feeling my storytelling. That usually helps my depression subside when I am offstage.

❀ Drag gives me something to work on and look forward to instead of just staying in bed. I can rhinestone, put outfits or music together.

❀ Every day I watch my very favorite performances. Even out of drag and not on stage watching the crowd go crazy and the love that I'm shown makes me cry happy tears. Drag helps me in so many ways even when I'm not on stage. It helped me find my people. It helped me find myself. It helped me come out as trans.

❀ Much of my time I treat my living room as a stage when I am not booked in a show. I can get some of the emotions out especially if it is between bookings. Even being on stage and doing drag is not a 100% cure for depression, but it helps make it bearable.

❀ After realizing that this is my passion, working on things for my drag often helps me. The thing that gives me the most happiness is entertaining, educating, inspiring, and provoking thought in others. I am going through the process of doing that when creating a piece of art: a lip-sync, costume, a music mix, a performance, et cetera. I get really excited just thinking about the end result. The thought of the happiness that I can create for others helps me replace my depressive episodes with something that gives me joy.

Chapter Six, Question Six
"How does dressing up
help you to deal with depression?"

❦ Sometimes when I don't have a show, I dress up. No, I am not a crossdresser. I dress up to check out my outfits. Do they still fit? Do they inspire me? I practice my make up. I spoil my wigs. I organize my closet. I clean my makeup. I get out of my black space by giving it optimistic thoughts. I listen to songs. Can I picture myself do this song? When I am very depressed it is hard to start this list of things to do. My voice tells me to put it all in a box and walk away. This is when I know I need to do it the most, when I want it the least.

❦ Getting into face always helps me after a long hard day of work even if I have a show or not. Sometimes life as (my boy-name) isn't as exciting as life as (my DRAG name). If my boy-name had a bad day then my DRAG persona has always been there to cheer me up. If it wasn't for my DRAG persona, I wouldn't have the drag family I have and without my drag family I wouldn't have friends. Makeup has been a part of my expression and getting into full geish* allows me to provide that escape. Even if it is just for a little two hour show or if it's just to cook dinner and do the dishes.

Geish: (origin: geisha) Drag makeup and wardrobe. As when Vivacious says, "Gia is still a ladyboy, in or out of geish."

❦ Not only do I dress for the stage but I continue to dress for who I am off stage. During the year of doing drag, I found myself. I was meant to be a woman.

❦ Sometimes it just feels good to just be someone else for a moment.

❦ I think "faking it until you make it" holds some truth. I do feel better if I get dressed rather than staying in pajamas all day. Sometimes I just don't feel up for getting into drag, but other times I let my emotions fuel my art. I create new looks and end up feeling good about what I've done.

❦ I do think it helps. Follow the infamous quote, "be the change." You can't put yourself in a better head space if you aren't doing anything to attempt to alter it. Envisioning yourself in a happy place is extremely helpful to me. Imagining yourself in a costume performing a song you love in your bedroom in front of the mirror is soul joy to me!

❀ I feel like I am someone else when I perform. I get to live my life as someone completely different and act any way I want. I do not care what people think of me or how they see me. I can be a complete clown and smile ear to ear. And for days when I'm not performing, I can just get dressed up for fun and film some videos and practice taking my mind off of the rest of the world.

❀ Dressing up transforms me to a different world. Drag, to me is not just musical, it's acting, which allows the performer to be someone totally different. When I am dressed fully in drag I feel free. Free to give myself permission to smile for a change. It is a very liberating experience. One thing that happens for me is when I am in drag as a King I have a very silly personality. I am quite the joker! When I dress as Diva, I can finally pretend to be a wealthy woman. Classy and very demure. Although sometimes it is kind of fun to be a loosy goosey. I escape my reality. All of the bruises and cuts from my past disappear. The harsh words in my memory bank turn into puffs of smoke. The desire to enter the atmosphere as a spirit flies away. I am creating my monument. I do have difficulty with those who feed on dealing out ire filled words, and the drama that comes with Drag is sometimes very hard. I think some people do not realize that the things they say can hurt more then any bodily pain one can inflict. Whether it be jealousy, or projections of pain the person feels, it is evident that those people simply do not remember how they feel when it happens to them. I try to not allow it to break my bubble of joy, but sometimes I have to do my make up over again from sitting in the bathroom crying.

❀ I tend not to dress up on days I'm not performing, but I do rehearse and mentally block my acts. Having a sense of purpose helps me come up with a reason to take care of myself through the day.

❀ Dressing up helps a ton with my depression even when I'm not going on that stage. When I lay down that makeup on my face and see the angles change, seeing my face finally take on that full masculine physique, my entire body and mind lightens. Taking the extra time to dress up and paint my face also gives me a slight grounding moment, a moment where my brain has to concentrate on one task instead of flying around like a squirrel which also helps in calming the depression. Finally, when I'm depressed and get dressed up, my entire mood lightens because I finally feel like and look like the "pretty goth boy" I want to be every single day, but am too scared to be.

❀ Getting in drag gives me focus and gives me euphoria when I'm down.

❀ Getting in drag gives me focus and gives me euphoria when I'm down.

❀ I've always been in planning mode prior to days of my performances. Concentrating on my drag shows keeps my mind occupied and away from my depression. I make lists of music so as not to repeat songs from day to day. I take time to reflect on past performances and the costumes I've worn previously. I tend to beat myself up pertaining to past performances if the audiences didn't like or approve of my selections or of what I wore. Wardrobe malfunctions happen but I try to prevent them at all costs. I get anxious wanting the crowd to like what I'm presenting all the time, including what I'm saying on a microphone. I do try to hide my depression because I'm there to uplift and entertain others as best I can. I allow myself to interact with the audience as I'm there for their entertainment and keep the show upbeat. I've been very successful masking my depression, after all, I'm an actor.

❀ Getting dressed helps me get into character which in turn takes me away from real world. I am a completely different person when I'm in drag.

❀ To me drag is a costume, a mask to hide behind; I become someone stronger and braver. I can turn into a person that even my friends no longer see "me." It allows me to be free, my mind to breath and my soul to relax. When in drag I no longer live by the rules my life and surroundings have placed on my shoulders. I no longer must fit into the perfect mold... I am a King!

❀ Music and costuming definitely helps me with depression when I'm not on stage. My fiancée makes me listen to the mixes. I let myself get lost in it and picture me doing them. It definitely has helped me in many ways.

❀ Taking the time to get my songs ready and my drag outfits forces me to get out of my head. The thoughts that when I do perform, my drag family will be there for hugs and support. I do not even have to say how I am feeling. They give hugs and positive energy to me without even knowing if I'm having a really crazy day. It gives me that thought, just one more day, and I will be with my family.

❀ For a brief moment of time I don't have to feel like me. When dressing up I can feel like someone else. Everything seems right in the world and my depression is gone for a bit. By time I hit the stage I feel like a completely different person and I'm ready to take on the night. If I don't have a show, getting in costume still helps me work out many problems.

❀ If I go to a show that I'm not performing in, dressed up in DRAG and someone recognizes me or asks about my drag, it makes me feel important. I matter because even for a brief moment I am not myself-- the real me.

❀ The dressing is always my last stage. Usually by the dressing stage, my head is clear. The paint is what helps me the most of the time. If I'm dancing in the show, the warming up really boosts endorphins big time.

❀ I always feel a bit better when I know I look nice. When you get compliments that goes even farther, but my favorite is when I'm on stage and I hear someone talking about my outfit to their friends. I know I'm doing it right and also feels very validating that someone sees the effort I put in.

❀ I have a ritual when getting "dressed up". During this time, I transform into my drag persona. He doesn't have any cares, other than to make the crowd happy and feel invited. I do not dress up on any other days except show days. It helps having multiple shows to perform in. On the days I do not dress up, and I am feeling enough energy, I try to spend time crafting my outfits. This also keeps my mind off of my depression.

❀ You feel better when you look good. Also, I keep my body in motion. Motion creates emotion! I yell and stomp around to get pumped up on the music or on occasion a stress cry. It's so important to enter the stage without eight million things on your mind. I was a Marine and my battalion rolled out to the song, "Bodies" by Drowning Pool. I still use that song. It's key to me performing now because I have a superstition about rolling to a gig without it. This piece takes me immediately back to pumping up before combat. It still works for me.

❀ The reaction of the audience always effects my performance, the more they like it the better I feel I did, so for me it is about getting my outfit complete. I feel pretty and it is useful to my depression.

❀ My drag persona has allowed my younger self to live vicariously. My stage persona is the person you would have seen when I was twenty-something. Bringing them to life on stage has now crossed over to real life reality. My external self is finally catching up with my internal self. The more I do drag the faster I am becoming the person I love to see in the mirror.

❀ I don't practice anywhere before I do shows. I'm not what you would call a pretty girl in makeup. When I go on stage, I basically play the fool and have a great time. When I go to the bar and step into the dressing room, I become a completely different person. I know this sounds cliche but as soon as I set at my makeup mirror it's like a dark cloud has been lifted. Normally I am very shy in social settings but when I'm in Drag I become sassy and love making people laugh. The free liquor probably helps. That's a topic for another time. I am lucky to have a great drag family. When my depression is a problem, they seem to be able to sense it. They're always there for me and to cheer me on. When I'm not doing shows I can work on my costumes to keep my mind off from things. I take medication for my depression, but I don't find they really help so I skip them. They actually can interfere with my drag sometimes. It's funny how I never thought about much of this stuff until this book.

❀ Drag is a break from my daily struggles. A break from reality. When I'm not dressed or performing, I often listen to the music I like to perform. There is a song for everything and a song can change your whole outlook, even if it is only temporary. Shopping for drag is also a positive experience for me. The planning and gathering of things for a particular look or performance is always fun. It is a chance to let go of my depression triggers.

❀ I'm very reserved as a boy. My female persona allows me to express myself in ways that boy me could never do and it brings so much joy to my heart. All the work that goes into a performance can take me there. Shopping, rehearsing, and music brings me up!

❀ Simply dressing up in Drag any day can brighten my mood. I especially enjoy the change of character and vibe on my off days of performing which always helps to boost my spirits when needed. I typically take a before and after picture when I get in face and costume so I have physical proof to show myself that I did something impactful that day. I also make it a point to spend quality time with myself in the mirror when I'm in full face. It always reminds me of how far I've come from knowing literally nothing about makeup to teaching others makeup application techniques I've acquired over the years. I think off days are some of the most important because you have time to experiment with new looks which leads you to a deeper understanding of your character. When I'm struggling with my depression on show days, I always take time to myself, staring in the mirror, saying specific positive phrases out loud to myself that I find to be particularly inspiring and empowering. I also always have my favorite blues tunes that have helped me heal from trauma in the past playing in the background while show prepping.

❀ When I dress up, I feel myself completing my transformation into my superhero self. I don't really dress up on days when I don't perform but I do put on extravagant makeup on off days. I also perform lip sync every single day. This acts as a muscle that I need to work out and I'm constantly learning new things as I rehearse.

❀ When I transform it's like I feel free. What's on my shoulders before is no longer on my shoulders. I look different feel different with a different kind of attitude. My depression is put on the back burner and I have new thoughts, new attitude and I use that to push me forward. Depression is part of life but if a dress in bright colors can make me happy, I put it on.

❀ For me I live everyday as me on stage or not. The only difference is when I perform, I look as close at the artist I'm imitating. I pay close attention to every move from their videos.

❀ When I dress in drag, my performing character comes to the surface. It provides both a distraction and a reprieve from what I deal with on a daily basis. It feels like telling my depression that I'll get back to it in a few hours, and shutting the door. It's not gone, but it's not following me around. I can breathe, and focus, and socialize in a way that I'm not able to in my daily life.

❀ Depression for me these days comes partly from my appearance. I'm getting older, and I can really tell. My hair is sparingly thin and whenever I wear makeup the wrinkles make it crease like crazy. My nails have started to grow in weird. I feel very subconscious going anywhere in the world in my "normal" attire. Actively trying to be better at just loving myself the way I am, but it is definitely hard. Especially when your job is literally being looked at. When I dress up for the stage, I finally feel beautiful again. Wigs hide the head, and enough makeup to try and cover up. The flashy costumes make me feel glamorous. I feel like I enjoy looking at myself again, and I feel confident when others are looking. I do have to remind myself though that everything is just an accessory, that I'm still the same person underneath it and capable of being beautiful. I've started to take some of those into my daily life. I wear wigs out, because who really cares? I wear clothing sometimes that people might find 'eccentric'. I feel lovely in them, and in the end, I'm dressing up for me, and not for others.

❦ In the beginning drag was a mask for me to be able to go into places my anxiety wouldn't let me. After a few times on stage, I got it. It was what I was born to do. I just happened to have lived in a place where drag was seen as unimportant. I didn't let people who kept telling me I couldn't do it to stop me.

❦ Dressing up helps me change my mindset. I can alter the lens that I am looking through to engage the world. It allows me a moment of breathability, grounding and existence.

❦ Dressing up always makes me feel better about myself. It definitely makes me feel a million times better. When I look good and have on a costume my outlook of myself is definitely a high. I can then look on the mirror and sometimes say "Wow, I really look good!" When I see pictures sometimes, I can't believe I looked that good. It does wonders for my self-esteem.

❦ It honestly gives me a different form of confidence when I dress up as my drag persona and not as myself. My drag persona has confidence and his confidence is attractive. Nothing can touch him. I'm hoping one day that his confidence will pass over to me. He's a mask for me and one day I'm hoping to be able to 100% commit to him and be myself. But right now, dressing up as my alter ego he can be my support system and making me feel more confident in my sad fits of depression.

❦ As with any character I play on a stage, it is a release because you get a chance to be someone else for a split second in time. Before going on stage, you get a rush of adrenaline, a nervousness, and wave of excitement that is all uncontrollable. These all help you cope and focus on things other than your depression. When I am not performing and get struck with depression I try to focus on my main focus, spreading joy to others!

❦ Dressing up helps me to deal with depression both before I go on stage and on days when I have no performances by allowing me to have the sense of control over how I choose to present myself. Part of my depression is struggling with my gender identity. I identify as gender fluid. When I'm in a pessimistic headspace suffering from imposter syndrome, I will practice my DRAG makeup, work on my upcoming dance routines, or go to my closet and piece new costumes together; it helps me to reflect and reaffirm who I know I am. I use dressing up as a time to escape my mental status by adopting the mannerisms and personality of the character based on the wardrobe choice at the time. For example, if I feel like I need a confidence boost, I will wear my dapper gentleman or leather daddy costume in order to feel a surge of suave and swagger.

❀ Dressing up gives me the opportunity to become a different person for those few minutes. It also allows me to try different ways to approach a dilemma. What question is the character dealing with in the song. How would I normally handle it? What is a different way to approach it? Dressing up helps me to become a different person by trying it on temporarily.

❀ Dressing up helps me get into character or at least feel the confidence of my persona. Usually, my drag clothes are my everyday masculine clothing, so it's more about feeling masculine, but with that same confidence. Before performances, it also just takes away another stressor for getting ready.

❀ I practice on days I'm not performing because a professional always perfects the craft. It's an escape because I can only focus on a fun and exciting experiences to enrich someone else's lives for a moment.

❀ Dressing up helps me feel good.

❀ When I dress, I become my stage persona, and he is happy, jolly, funny and makes others laugh, even myself. I feel my persona is so helpful in my depression. I never know what is going to come out of his mouth!

❀ I have never been one to rehearse or practice. I am very much an in the moment, improv performer, which often means I do not "finalize" a performance until I start packing for a show. In workshops I teach, I explain how I often prepare for a show with nothing more than my music and a mirror that I position so that only my face is visible. I do this because when I decide on a song, I challenge myself to convey my message using only my facial expressions. Eyes are a very underutilized, yet powerful tool when it comes to connecting with an audience. If I can tell my entire story, concerning any given song, using just my eyes and facial expressions, then everything else I do simply amplify the impact I can make on others and that is what helps overpower the depression.

❀ Dressing up helps me try to bring the image I have in my head to life. I also practice for upcoming shows and reflect on previous performances to help future ones.

❀ I practice my dance moves and memorizing my songs at home. Trying on outfits for the music I have chosen gives me something to focus on. It takes over my mind where my depression starts.

❀ Dressing up helped me learn to do my daily makeup as a trans woman. This helped with the dysphoria and my confidence in who I am as a woman.

❀ Getting ready to perform use to be to show how I saw myself and felt and now as a Female to Male (FTM) it's brought out confidence and humility and helped me stand tall. Newfound confidence is sexy!

❀ Getting into drag is transformational for me. Sometimes I literally feel like another person, especially when my makeup is on point! The process helps to pull me out of whatever I was thinking and forces me to focus on my craft instead. I really appreciate drag for doing that for me.

❀ Getting dressed in my drag makes me feel like I'm putting on a mask. It is why I make my contour in the way it's shaped. When I become my drag persona, I am confident and having fun. I love the way my costumes and clothing make me feel. I feel sexy, and cool; I feel so excited.

❀ Dressing up in drag allows me to create a fictional character and simultaneously be my truest self. This empowers me to combat depression every day of my life.

❀ Dressing up and fulfilling the passion is such a great relief. I am not a number in a conformed world. I love my female side and embrace it to the max. Wearing flats or heels, with nylons and expressing the Queen is amazing and of insight. Its passionate.

❀ Dressing up makes me feel more confident and pretty. I sometimes dress up when I feel depressed, just to make myself feel better.

❀ Dressing up for me allows me to choose things that make me more confident in myself. I often battle gender and body dysmorphia being a baby, trans man, pre-top surgery. Being able to dress hyper masculine allows me to feel like a man. It is something that always makes me better.

❀ Dressing up for me becomes a challenge to me by making a costume creation that goes with the nightly theme. I want to stand out as someone that they will remember so they will ask about me the next time they come out to that venue.

❀ I like to joke that my outfits are like superhero armor. When I put on a face and whatever sparkly outfit I'm wearing that day, it's like the rest of the non-drag world disappears. I become confident and am able to do things I can't do in my day-to-day life. It doesn't mean it actually disappears. I may still be anxious or depressed, but it's almost like I can choose to push it to the side and pretend it is gone for a couple hours.

❀ Dressing for shows or just every day for me is about making yourself happy. If I am wearing something that I like it helps me to look at myself in a different manner. This helps me when I am depressed.

Chapter Seven, Question Seven
"How does performing help you deal with depression?"

❀ Look at the lady in the front row, she is smiling so hard. There is love in the eyes of this man trying to hand me a dollar. Oh wait, this is the part of the song where I outstretch my arms and belt out the song. The spotlight seems brighter tonight but I can still hear the audience clapping and cheering. So many thoughts going through my head. I don't have time to worry about some clown that made me feel bad on social media. I don't have time to think of rent being late. I am in my zone and there is no room for depression.

❀ In the moment, you become someone else while performing, you personify your drag personality, and it distracts you. It can make you feel like you really make a difference, especially in a place you are enjoyed and loved for who you are!

❀ During my time on stage, nothing in the real-world matters. I am a different person. I'm in my own concert and that's all I think about. My drag persona isn't the one dealing with my troubles.

❀ Depending on the music I'm performing that night. It will either lets me put on the "fake it 'til you make it" mask and flat out ignore the depression at hand or it allows me to lean into the depression, leave it all on the stage and walk away from the performance feeling a touch happier than when I walked in.

❀The feedback of applause and tips from the audience validates me.

❀ It truly changes my perception of my depression for 2.5 minutes. For that small window I feel completely free of my depression. Truly no greater hit to my depression then getting on stage and turning a number!

❀ Performing gives me something to look forward to each week. I can plan my numbers and my costumes, which gives me something to do. On the day of performance, even if I don't really feel like doing it, I can push through knowing I don't want to let anyone down. The social interactions and energy from the crowd generally gets me feeling better afterward.

❀ Performing helps me put my emotions on stage and into whatever song I'm doing. When I'm going through a hard time, I choose a song that reflects how I'm feeling and put all of the emotions that are inside of me into that performance. It helps me be who I am and show my true feelings and emotions which takes all the pressure of the depression off of me.

❀ My brain entirely switches off during performance. It's all muscle memory and reaction to what the audience does. I think it helps reset my brain.

❀ Performing keeps me focused on the music and the audience. My depression goes away when the audience is clapping.

❀ I have some acts that help me process my depression or things connected to it.

❀ I pick a song or songs to match how I am feeling. It helps to relieve the pressure depression puts on my mind, a cry for help that I have too much weight on my shoulders. I can't be the only one carrying it.

❀ Jumping onto the stage, everything I was going through before is out the window, even if for only that time. Now it's just me, the audience, and the music. It's like everything got washed away. I end up leaving the stage happy, as if whatever was bothering me is gone.

❀ When I hit the stage, I can feel the love. I do camp drag so everyone is laughing and having a great time. Just knowing people love me is so good for my depression. For those three or four minutes it's like the old me is sucked out of my head. The adrenaline rush is so strong my arthritis pain actually disappears during the performance. When the pain is at its worse, I perform with a walker and the audience eats it up. You have to work with what you got. When I step off the stage, I generally can't remember what I did unless I see a video. Weird huh?

❀ When I hear the emcee start to talk me up I get an adrenaline rush. When my music starts, I immediately transform into my drag persona and become a totally different person. My drag persona is confident, beautiful, mysterious and a fierce entertainer. For a few minutes all is well in my little world as the joy in my heart is immeasurable. When a fan comes up to thank me after a number, I know exactly why they did so... I saved a life.

❀ When I'm onstage I can feel my sadness and worries disappear because I know I'm in a place where I am safe, loved, and accepted.

❀ When in drag I can feel my depression starting to melt away in a sense. It gives me hope once again and everything doesn't feel so dark.

❀ Performing is therapy. It's a chance for my regular self and my stage persona to join forces and fight whatever the issue of the day is in a way that I otherwise couldn't fight. The crowd knows when you're going through something real instead of just dancing around to the latest top forty pop-tart. They experience it with you if you do it right.

❀ For me it's when I'm my stage persona, I'm not me. I'm not the nonbinary human depressed. I'm my stage persona, a confident happy-steal-your-girl man. I get fully into persona and have a surplus of spoons. I don't have enough spoons to get through my day as me.

❀ Performing is a way for me to not only connect with others who let me know I'm not alone or unwanted, but it also helps me process and release everything that I'm feeling. Every time I step off stage, I feel a little of the weight lifted off my shoulders. While I'm performing, I can be sad, I can be angry, I can be scared and I will still be safe even in my vulnerability. It is unbelievably freeing to be able to express yourself in such a raw and open manner, even though it's only for a few minutes.

❀ Performing is an outlet; a way to say or feel the things I normally would hide. Leading up to my performance I am a bundle of nerves, but once I step out on that floor and the spotlight hits me, I am "in the zone". While in drag and performing the depression melts away. I can let all the emotions leave my brain through my song choices. I like to say I am able to "leave it all on the floor" and walk back into the dressing room with a small bit of emotional closure.

❀ Doing drag usually helps me to deal with my problems and lots of issues. It gives me freedom to express myself and to be able to drown out my sadness with rejection.

❀ I think performing on the stage in front of supportive, high-energy crowds are honestly some of the best experiences I've ever had in life! The flood of endorphins I experience while in the spotlight never fails to elevate my mood. My acts are almost always political or hold meaningful messages to share with the crowd so the act of performing them on stage are both incredibly cathartic and rewarding. A few current acts, namely my "Abortion Rights" and "Gay Agenda" mixes, help alleviate the anxiety and depression I feel each time I read the news about the endless anti-LGBTQ+ legislation and overturning of Roe v Wade." I release my anger and frustration on the stage and create an environment for the audience to also feel those overwhelming emotions so we can hold space for each other and process them together. This is such a powerful platform for performance artists to channel their frustration or sadness into an empowering piece of art. Not only does it spark an emotional response from the audience, but also helps you heal along the way. Drag continues to teach me how to process queer oppression through humor, hence "the Gay Agenda."

🏵 I get a rush and high by being on stage. Performing to me is a meaningful use of my time and energy where I help impact other people's realities in a positive way. Knowing that I have a performance to look forward to helps give me reason to live.

🏵 It can literally give me the ability to come out of a deep depression. The whole experience from making all my stuff to planning the performance and doing the performance live releases all the stuff built up in me.

🏵 Performing is a great way for me to feel seen. For three to six minutes, I can be whoever and whatever I want to be on stage! I like to perform at venues where the people love drag and everyone gets love. From the most seasoned, to the newest ingénue. It's so great to make connections with the audience. I feed off of the energy. It gives me life! Not to mention all the lovely compliments.

🏵 Performing makes me happy because I'm bringing joy to the people at the shows. I find depression is nowhere around me.

🏵 When I am on stage, I feel wholly and completely seen. As an artist, as a queer person, as an intersex individual. I feel beautiful, creative, and desired. I am able to get out pent up energy, express emotions, and convey a story. It holds me accountable for getting out of my bedroom. It makes sure I eat so that I have energy. It forces me to take care of my hygiene. All of this is why performing is my life blood.

🏵 Performing doesn't always help me with my depression to be fully honest. I tend to disassociate during my performances and rarely remember what I have actually done. The disassociation is a normal response for me. I have been told by my therapists that this is due to the stress and anxiety from putting myself out there in a vulnerable way by performing. Being on stage in front of people is a vulnerable place. It is you alone with a bunch of people facing you that can react in good or bad ways which causes a space of vulnerability as you never know how they will react. This is why I will usually try to create collaborative performances with others as I tend to not disassociate when I am with others on stage. I will still do single performances to continue to help with myself growth and resilience.

❀ Performing helps my depression by giving me a place to let everything out safely. By putting my emotions and feelings into a performance, I find that my head is able to clear, and I feel the weight of the world come off my shoulders for a minute. Oh! We cannot forget the "rockstar" feeling I get when I hear my name announced and the crowd scream for me. Who could be depressed with adoring fans, family and friends cheering them on? I know I can't be depressed! That crowd's energy gives me a reason to keep coming back to the stage, and gives me a reason to live.

❀ Still being new at being a Drag King I have realized it when I put on my makeup costume. I see the guests watch my performances, it puts me in a totally different place and I don't think about the things that are going on in my life. Being another "me", helps me learn the real me.

❀ Performing puts me in a whole different world. The worries of the world are gone once I hit the stage. I have no care on the world except the song mix I'm performing once I hear the introduction of my name. I step on that stage and feel the music and crowd. It will usually put me in complete euphoria.

❀ It helps me get out of my shell and forces me to get out of bed, in a good way. It keeps my mind moving and not stuck idling so I keep overthinking. When my brain has other things to think about, I have a moment of a clear blue sky. When I perform, I get a rush of natural dopamine and I feel my art makes people happy. I was in a show when I met my beautiful girlfriend at a show. It wouldn't have happened if I didn't get out of my bed. It wouldn't have happened if mt stage persona wasn't there. So many happy things come out of doing drag and it's such a beautiful thing. Filled with beautiful hearted people.

❀ The stage is my opportunity to grow in my mental victories. To embrace what makes me different than others and contribute to building confidence in those that see my show. Depression for me is not a once fixed always fixed. It is a form of response conditioning that allows us to overcome hurdles a bit more effectively. Depression has taught me to celebrate people where they are, on the way to where they are going.

❀ Performing and feeling the energy from the audience always brings me so much joy and happiness. As my female persona, I can take a break from my every day struggles and only focus on her!

❀ Being a live singing queen, helps me so much because performing is my passion. I love entertaining people; it gives me so much joy, especially using my talents as an outreach by giving my testimony of where I have been and what I have been through. I grew up in a religious home and tried to help others to not have to feel the way others made me feel.

❀ Performing helps me deal with depression by allowing me to have a disconnect from the part of my psyche which causes negative thoughts and emotions. Once the music begins, a different part of my brain takes over and I focus on the song lyrics and my choreography. It helps me to get out of my head and let loose with whichever persona I decide to embody during the routine.

❀ Performing helps me by keeping me looking in a forward direction. If I have performances, outfits and makeup to plan, I don't get lost in my negative thoughts. Every day that I plan ahead helps to keep me in the here and now.

❀ For me, I feel your mood shifts based on what you feed it. Performing puts me around people enjoying themselves, whether it be fellow entertainers or spectators. In turn, that often brings me back to the light!

❀ By becoming a different person, I get to escape the mental breakdown of myself. I am able to explore the love and amazing experience of the female persona.

❀ I get to channel someone else and interact with a generally happy audience.

❀ I look forward for drag, it causes me to focus on my choreography, music and costumes, I also produce shows, so I get to work with new artists who need coaching and costume design help and seasoned artists who want guidance on the crowds and what they enjoy. Once I am on the stage it is all about entertaining, and that releases endorphins and endorphins make you happy.

❀ I have a very hard time opening up to others. This is in part due to me being an empath. I am often inundated with the emotions of others, so that I have no bandwidth left to process my own. Drag is my way of opening up and communicating feelings I find difficult to put into words.

❀ I was a musician so it kind of feels like my job. I have the freedom to pick anything I want song-wise and clothes. It is really cool because you can just be yourself. It's self-empowering.

❀ I start to focus on the music and forget all about my problems. It just feels good that there are people who want to see the work and effort I put into my performance.

❀ I get to disappear into the world of art and performing. It is exciting and interesting so that keeps me and my mind busy in a happy environment. It doesn't give me time to be depressed.

❀ Once I am in full drag and preparing to go on stage that is all I can think about. Every dollar I make during a performance goes back to local non-profit organizations in my community. I am super focused on doing the best I can during a performance so I feel it just doesn't leave room for depression to take over, at least not in that moment.

❀ The high I get from seeing people rocking out and just forgetting their troubles for five minutes is such a rush; it makes me forget my own problems.

❀ Love being able to express what's going on. I love to see and feel what people get out of my performance or the others I am sharing the stage with. Nothing better to see a smile or a tear from someone coming up to me to say, "I needed that" or how it made them feel. Performing is part of why I do what I do!

❀ Performance in general is such a creative outlet - there should be much great thought behind each routine and number. The more time you take to make your performance the best it can be the more time you have away from depression. Searching for a new song or a mix of sound bites hopefully takes you out of your current state and into fun. Striving for the best and making it a reality can be very cathartic, especially when the audience enjoys what you have displayed before them.

❀ For me, drag is like being in art therapy. It allows me to focus on something when I get ready instead of the bad. I'm able to let go and express myself when I perform - especially when it's a number that I view as a therapeutic piece.

❀ It's almost like a blur, sounds, noises and faces. I feel the excitement of the crowd. I feel the music and the audience fuels me. Letting loose feels amazing. The fact that the audience is sharing this moment with me is so amazing.

❀ Seeing the reactions of others when I am in drag brings me such joy. This is such an antidote to the darkest days of my depression.

❀ The audience and sisters that see me perform on stage, DJ or host sets me up for a better aura performing. Music from artists or other amazing drag queens puts me in a better mood. Performing is therapy for me.

❀ Performing allows me to express my emotions in a healthy way that people can relate to. I put every ounce of emotion into the lyrics of every song I do. I'm definitely doing a ballad if I feel sad. If I feel seductive, you're going to get seduction! Et cetera, et cetera. Being able to get those emotions out frees my mind a bit and allows me to get out of that depression state I'm in.

❀ When I am on a stage and spotlights are on me... I feel like a superstar. I have everyone's attention watching and enjoying me on that stage.

❀ Performing helps me deal with my depression by allowing me an outlet to express my feelings that I'm not always comfortable doing in life. Music has always been a type of therapy for me so being able to choose songs that resonate with me, to use them to express myself helps me deal with life and clear my head. Bonus when it touches an audience member and helps them as well.

❀ The attention helps me focus on the audience and not myself. It gets me out of my head and feelings. It allows me to relax and be in the moment. It allows me to just let loose and be myself if only for a few hours.

❀ Honestly, it makes me perform my heart out. I want to feel like I've made an impact on the people watching me perform. I want to feel like I left a good memory and that I was remembered for something I'm proud of.

Chapter Eight, Question Eight
"How does social media, as your DRAG persona, help you deal with depression?"

❀ The worse thing you can do is think social media is your friend. Too many people rely on social media for their feedback. They are addicted to refreshing their page to see if anyone is interacting with them. They are trolling other pages comparing themselves to other entertainers often forgetting that those people most likely only post the best of themselves. Everybody has bad days. You don't have to have depression to feel like a failure. Take the love you get from social media. Discount the negative. They don't pay your rent... well unless you are letting them live in your head rent free.

❀ I originally avoided social media like the plague, but it became an off-stage area to express my sense of humor, my politics, and to teach the young people about gay history.

❀ I'm only on social media as my persona. It helps me to see people love me no matter what's happening.

❀ Social media can either make me or break me. In most cases, my friends and fans help me stay uplifted. But occasionally, negativity reaches me and it can feed my depression. It's rare though. I have different pages from my everyday page to my drag persona pages and it helps me cut that down.

❀ By the time social media was hitting and hitting big, the line between my drag persona and myself was blending big time. It really helped me speak openly about my depression and anxiety. The biggest thing is that social media has helped de-stigmatized mental health.

❀ Social media is fun which helps bring me pleasure. It's nice also having an escape from everyday reality and it's like a platform for my superhero alter ego to express herself.

❀ My Drag persona presence on social media has significantly contributed to my ability to be vulnerable with others about my depression and anxiety. I'm naturally more confident in face so I think it makes it easier for me to share intimate details about my life with the world. Social media can be a platform that builds community for those struggling with multifaceted mental illnesses. Sharing personal experiences through stories, posts, or reels really helps to connect and relate to people from all around the world having similar struggles with depression. My drag King page on Instagram has evolved into a space that encourages vulnerability, celebrates flamboyant authenticity, and shares mental health struggles hoping to be a resource for those on their gender discovery journeys. My drag king persona has helped me work through numerous depressive episodes and so, during lockdown I shared a music video I created about struggles with depression and suicide ideation. This led to comforting conversations with other queer folx who were dealing with similar mental health struggles. These interactions helped me feel less alone and more connected to my community. Hopefully my page can help make someone else feel less alone in this world.

❀ Today's social media is a great help. We are now able to share information and tips to find necessary things for our craft from jewelry, pads, even make up. I am old school, thirty years in the business, when things weren't so accessible.

❀ I keep my drag social media completely separate from my main personal account. It helps me to stay out of online debates and discussions on topics that might depress me.

❀ Social media has actually helped me connect with more fans and other drag artists. With new people rooting for me then aren't just my friends it gives me the serotonin I need to beat depression for a while. Tiktok and Instagram helps more over using Facebook.

❀ I tend not to get on social media when I'm depressed. I find social media can actually add to my depression because of all of the awful stuff going on in the world. When I not depressed, I like social media to stay in touch with friends and fan. I must say I get a lot of love from fans on my page.

❀ 98% of my social media stories are of drag persona rather than my personal self. Sharing my drag on social media allows me to share my vulnerability with the world. Keeping a strong social media presence and speaking my mind as my drag persona has helped my true self become more self-confident and effective in my day-to-day life.

❀ I had to take a long break from social media… over two years. I only recently came back and I'm still not sure it's the place for me. I support people I know and try to interact, but all social media does for me is remind that I am alone, invisible and forgotten. People used to respect their elder queens and appreciate what they've gone through and done for the community, but it's not like that way everywhere.

🌸 Social media for my drag persona can help with my depression because I'm not alone. I've made many connections to other performers with disabilities and I get to support other artists in my craft. I also get support in return.

🌸 Social media can be a hit or miss with drag. It's wonderful because the right hashtags can get you pretty far. You can be seen by people who only in your local area can see you. You get inspiration from other people and people can get inspiration from you. If I work really hard on a routine, I get really excited when I see people comment really nice things on my pictures or videos on social media. Makes me happy on days from feeling super down when I'm not 100% on my feet that day. Those little things can make a difference. Being "Liked" in a photo, sharing and showing your friends, commenting nice and loving words or even positive constructive criticism can really turn around someone's day especially mine. It's also helps me find local like-minded people. It's a great way to socialize, make friends and connections. Social media has definitely given me positives to rely on. You will always have those negative Nellies, but it's just as easy as deleting a comment.

🌸 I detest social media but after COVID hit it's now a new communication device. I've learned it's a necessary evil. I try hard to help my friends out. Now it's a tool. I can help more people and myself. Creating a win-win situation. Almost half my social media stories are advertising for others. I care deeply for this age-old art form.

🌸 I love my drag social media for my depression! I find it is the place that I go to most where I can take a break from all of me and be fully in my DRAG persona and nothing else. Not only is my drag social media where I can share things I do, but it is also a place that I have specifically created an echo chamber of amazing DRAG peeps (new and matured) to watch and learn from who are located all over the world. I learn so much from you all and it helps me push aside the depression.

🌸 Social media and drag have both given me platform to advocate loudly for mental health awareness, disability pride, trans equality and other important issues. An Australian drag legend told me at the start of my drag journey to wear the responsibility of drag with pride, that as drag artists we are the super heroes of the LGBTQIA + community, the first to be seen, the loudest, that it's our job to make ourselves seen and heard, so it's important that you've got something to say. Talking about depression and disability openly to a large audience through the lens of drag has been just as important and empowering to me as talking on it in private with my therapist. Community brings and binds us together, sharing our experiences spreads the message that no one is truly alone.

❀ Using my social media as my drag persona has opened up so many avenues. It gives me more platforms to share my art with the world and brings similar creators to me as well. Without social media, I would have never found my family and those individuals save my life over and over. Also, using social media as my drag persona allows me to grow my platform beyond a stage, which alleviates even more of my depression, as I am able to do what I love, in and outside of bars.

❀ Social Media is a great outlet for my creativity where I get the opportunity to share to the entire world. Creating videos and reaching others through social media helps me deal with my depression. It keeps me away from anything that's depressing to me.

❀ Social media is a good way to get exposure to connect with people from all sorts of different walks of life. Sometimes you can meet other people who are there to help pull you out of depression. You meet people who struggle the same as you do and it can be comforting to know that there are others like you who are making it happen. When you can't get out of bed, you can still socialize. It can also be a double-edged sword. People can be more vicious when they're hiding behind a computer screen. Sometimes all it takes is a quick negative comment that a person passing by will not ever even think about again. It can cause long lasting harm to the person they picked on that day. I have gone through multiple periods of my drag career where I can't even look at social media without it setting off triggers. It's harmful when it's the thing that makes you happy, but is also your source of income. Unfortunately, in this day and age social media is almost necessary to get bookings, so it affects your livelihood which in turn can affect your depression. You have to know when to walk away. Drag may be a character of yours, but it is still you behind the makeup, so be careful to balance the good as well as the bad.

❀ All the love and positive comments on social media can definitely put a smile on my face. Just spending time interacting with social media friends is sometimes all I need to brighten my day!

❀ The biggest help in social media was February 26, 2021 when I posted one my first TikTok video. I barely knew how to edit and it was choppy rough cuts, but I was just experimenting. I had done a version of This Is Me from the Greatest Showman and showed the many ugly words people can be called only to end in a power moment of my drag persona appearing. The next day I woke up to find my 2,000 followers had turned into 10k in a week. However, that wasn't the reason. The video was used to gain support for a gay guy who came out to his friends, who later that night tied his hands behind his back and beat him to death. The video was used to try to help get justice to label this a hate crime. Still to this day I try to make my drag to be a positive influence on others' lives, someway, somehow.

❀ My social media, as my DRAG persona, helps me deal with depression by allowing me to virtually interact with fans and other DRAG artists that I don't get to interact with in person on a daily basis. I am able to post my content, and get a positive interaction with my followers, which in turn, boosts my confidence and self-esteem.

❀ I don't think social media helps me. Someday it makes me more critical of myself. I see someone that sings instead of lip syncing. They pull together better outfits, moves and interact with the audience better. In the beginning social media seemed great thing for me. As it went on, it added to my depression and anxiety. I discovered that social media can actually be toxic for me. I can sink into a bad place by seeing things going on that I can't participate in or by seeing negative post or comments. It can really mess with my mental health. I've had to learn through therapy to not let social media determine my outlook on life. I truly see social media, for all the years that I've done drag, as a place to interact with club owners, show directors, my family and friends. I have to cautiously monitor my intake and use in order to have positive parts. For me it's much better to "not use it" than for it to cause me to go deeper into depression. That is self-care for me. I need to feel like I've done something worthwhile.

❀ It always helps when an audience member reaches out, posts photos or even comments on photos from shows they've attended and they express they had a good time. I always feel good!

❀ Having a social media account where I know I have to be professional whilst also being my "on brand wacky Drag Whatever-self" really helps me think about what I want to say carefully and helps me avoid doom scrolling on my personal account.

❀ My social media consists of friends and family. It is my oasis where love is always bountiful. It has truly consoled me at times. Although I have a tiny temper. When I see something that I feel strongly against I speak up.

❀ For me social media does not help with my depression at all. If anything, it makes it worse.

❀ Social media allows me to see life through my feminine side and escape the crazy world we live in.

❀ I only have one social media account and my drag name is my name. I don't bother looking at social media if it is filled with negativity and drama that day.

❀ Social Media is detrimental to my depression. Keyboard warriors have no idea what mental state you are in when they want to tell you that you are going to hell for being gay, that dressing in drag is a sin, et cetera. To me, social media is not a good outlet.

❀ This a bit complicated and simple at the same time. My stage persona and muggle self are deeply intertwined; I only have one online presence for all social media platforms. I deliberately choose not to separate the two online because the two are not entirely separate in my life offline. My stage persona is very much constructed from the same elements that make up my real-world identity. The two are delicately intertwined. When I am coping with depression-related issues I typically withdraw from social media and spend more time on my craft because it's drag that comforts, soothes, and restores me... not social media.

❀ Well I still study death and horror movies round the clock. Tic Watching TikTok videos help me. Horror movies uplift me, because someone has it worse than me. I've found many horror groups that do drag and horror. Had a conversation with my bestie on social media and learned how drag has exploded into all sorts of amazing and beautiful ways. Social media takes time and also when you're answering and talking to lots of people at the same time it is engrossing. I'm not a person who likes Facebook. I've only had an account for a year. Facebook probably helped people during this terrible pandemic. That's when I got into it. I met many great people and I talked to them.

❀ I just recently started to really use social media to help me escape from reality and not fall deeper into depression.

❀ I'm in my fifties, so social media is still something that I'm learning how to use. I try to post pictures of my persona after shows to see how they are viewed.

❀ Being on social media talking about my alter ego, my stage persona, makes me happy. I am happy talking or planning an upcoming event, discussing how to improve, tips from others or answering compliments. I also spend time looking and following at other drag performers on all different types of media. This seems to be a good form of reigning in on my depression.

❀ I post my photo shoots and TikToks and video of performances on mine and the love and positivity is amazing.

❀ It's the feedback I get from the community and other performers. TikTok has become a platform for many and I love it. I don't do drama; remarks uncalled for I ignore and remove. I try to stay positive, but also allowing myself to be vulnerable at moments.

❀ Social media plays a part because I can reach the community. It helps knowing beforehand who's showing up or excited to see me. That creates anxiety for me as well. I'm stoked to be on a post or flyer to be shared or commented on. I have a mouth of truth and can't help but spit things out. Brutal honesty has pulled me out of sad times when I see posts or even the people that posted about me. Makes me feel wanted and loved, not as unprofessional love, but I love some famous people too.

❀ I find interactions with others via social media to be equally encouraging and empowering. On days when my depression is darkest, it is these interactions that give me hope and light.

❀ I use different platforms on social media. I love to share with the Sisterhood both young and old of performing and valid advice. Drag is a passion and life for me. It depends on time which is fruitful to warm up and be ready when the event takes place. I created two pages alone on facebook. For original content there is TikTok.

✤ Social media has its ups and its downs with me as an artist. I love having so many supporters, fans and fellow drag artists to watch and love their work! At the same time these people are way more talented (or at least my brain tells me that I'm not as talented) and sometimes being on social media can tear me down.

✤ When I meet and greet with people that like my spirit and want pictures. I ask for people to add me as a friend on Facebook or Instagram and tag me. It makes me feel honored and happy when they do it.

✤ Social media is kind of a double-edged sword for me. I love when fans tag me, I love seeing other people's stuff and being inspired by it. At the same time, I spend way too much time comparing myself to other performers and how talented and polished they look and how my drag is worthless compared to everyone else. I also live in an area that is not super accepting outside of the drag community. I run a drag camp and story time for kids so I get lots of hate which I tend to take personally which only adds to the part of my brain telling me to quit so it can cause me to spiral.

✤ Social media has its ups and downs. People can be so critical of me which can put me further into depression. Other times it can be a great confidence booster. You never really know what's going to happen. Think about what you post and if you are emotionally able to handle everything that will come your way before you post anything.

✤ Realizing that there's people all over the world who love what I do and follow and interact with me is something that consistently makes my day. It's like there a whole bunch of people holding me accountable to the impact I make.

Chapter Nine, Question Nine
"People will assume that DRAG is a cure-all from depression. Can you explain if sometimes it does not work?"

❀ I blame drag sometimes when I am depressed. I blame myself. I blame others. I blame inanimate objects. I forget that the simplest things make me happy. I do not feel the love of others. I am overwhelmed. When I am at my worse, I don't know if I would read this book. I am in my own little world. I want to curl up and vanish. I need perceptive. DRAG is only a Band-Aid. A good one, but not a cure. When I get better, I will regret blaming everything, but not when I am in the crisis. I need something to blame.

❀ Drag definitely isn't a cure to depression all the times. Sometimes I start put on my makeup, stop and stare at the floor. I give up doing the makeup. Sometimes I even finish a makeup look and look in the mirror and realize that's still me. I look horrible. I wipe it off fast and try to redo it hoping it will help, when I realize it doesn't help, so I just give up for the day. It's hard when the depression is really overbearing.

❀ It often has the opposite effect because the adoration from the fans and friends, in many cases, is focused on your character rather than the real person behind the costumes and makeup. An entertainer's life can often be lonely because of that. You have to learn, often by being hurt, who is truly there for you and who is there for your "fame."

❀ All I can say is sometimes my brain will release the serotonin I need, other times I'm just sitting there in a costume and makeup feeling worse. Drag isn't a cure but it is like medicine it helps numb the depression. Personally, when feeling low and drag isn't helping, I reach out to the friends who I know have my back.

❀ I know that I have an endorphin release when doing my makeup and performing. If the audience is giving as much energy as I give out, I usually feel better but… this isn't something that always happens. Some crowds don't get what I'm doing or what the show is about. When that happens, it can pull me down. Also, when there is a lot of drama back stage or there is someone with an out-of-control ego, they can really pull me and others backstage down big time. They can take the air out of everyone.

❀ Sometimes the glitter and screaming crowd can make me forget I'm in a depression funk, but there are times where I walk off the stage feeling like all of my energy has been sucked out of me. I don't want to continue the shows anymore because my brain goes, "What's the point you'll never get anywhere with this, it's just a hobby you suck at, that eats up all your time and money?" From there I spiral. It could last anywhere from minutes to hours to even days.

❀ Nothing will ever be easy for me. That's something I learned recently. I have to work very hard to maintain my health, both physical and mental and sometimes drag can take a toll on both of those things. When I'm feeling good, I can't take it for granted because I do lots of work to feel good and stay feeling good, and there are a lot of other reasons besides drag that help me get there.

❀ Drag for me, isn't a cure all. It's a fabulous Band-Aid that generally does the trick but sometimes I get in such a funk nothing works. I have talked with other queens about this subject and we all agreed that drag is a huge help with depression, but get professional help if you think it will help. If you're on medication take them. They don't work if they sit in the medicine cabinet.

❀ While drag is a huge help for my depression, it is absolutely not a cure. It only temporarily takes my mind off if it. Once the show is over, I have to return to my real world. If you're depression gets unmanageable, seeking help may be the best option.

❀ There is no cure-all for mental illness, full stop. Drag, like any hobby or side gig, certainly can help my depression; nothing can cure my depression or any of my mental illnesses. Drag can certainly distract me from whatever I may be feeling and it may help to have somewhere to get that depressive energy out in a healthy way, but it doesn't help forever. That's why it's important to get the help you need; therapy, medication, or at least a strong support system.

❀ Nothing is a cure all. Allow yourself to be happy whether by a look, inspiration or creation. If you are still depressed, change until you are no longer depressed. Depression happens but when things don't work your way rework everything until you are happy.

❀ It's doesn't always cure sad feelings. It is like medication; it works for a while, but sometimes you get used to it and it doesn't give you the relief that used to give you. That's totally ok. You Just have to switch things up. Find something else to perform that will cause you a little bit more joy, something that excites you. If you're down that's totally alright. I have days where I'm super excited for a performance. I'm super excited because I put so much detail and plan into the outfits, look, and music. Sometimes the day of the show I get put into a pit of sadness and anxiety. It is totally ok to feel that way. If we all knew something bad was going to happen the next day we wouldn't go outside. Drag and life are roller coasters. We just have to enjoy the highs and lows of the ride.

❀ Depression and its cures often fail, which includes doing drag. Drag is not a cure all. There's no aspirin for that headache. I smoke enough pot to disconnect from it . It's side effect of changing your point of view, is good. You will want to eat and pass out before you take yourself seriously about suicidal ideation.

❀ I think it's crucial that we make it blatantly clear that Drag is not a cure-all from depression. While drag has the capacity to bring significant joy into your life in many facets that by no means equates to a cure from depression. In my experience drag has greatly improved the quality of my life especially with contributing to a better understanding of my gender identity and boosting self-confidence, but it's important to recognize that I still struggle with major depression every day. I still unfortunately suffer from the debilitating symptoms of depression despite having a therapist, psychiatrist, depression medication, a wonderful emotional support system and passionately perform drag regularly. Drag may be one helpful form of treatment for depression but it cannot be the only method. I strongly encourage everyone to seek professional mental health care if you're experiencing symptoms of major depressive disorder (MDD) so you can make the best decisions for your health between you and your doctor.

❀ Drag is and never has been a cure all for my depression. It is one tool of many within my toolbox that I use to deal and process what is happening to me as well as to help create situations that may help increase brain chemistry that helps with my depression. What works for me may not work for others but it is important to navigate your health and depression with professional healthcare providers.

❀ The art itself isn't the antidepressant. It's light in the darkness and there is power and growth in self-expression, but it isn't a cure. There is no cure for a lifelong depression like mine. There is joy to be found in living though, and drag gave me another face to explore life through. In drag I found moments of joy, moments of powerful inspiration and self-expression, purpose, community, family, love and support; those things really do save lives.

❀ It's not always sunshine and rainbows doing drag. Being an entertainer can be tiring, sometimes very taxing on your ability, especially during a low episode. Sometimes you can have issues with makeup, mostly due to underlying anxiety, which makes you sweat and can cause makeup to run or even fail. The best thing you can do in those times is take some extra time so that you're not as pressured.

❀ Drag is definitely not a cure-all from depression. You're still the same person you were before that makeup went on when that makeup comes off. Your problems don't just magically disappear because you've been in makeup or a cute outfit for a while. Sometimes my favorite hobby is also my worst enemy if I find that I've overbooked myself. It puts an intense strain on my mental health and sometimes causes breakdowns. Drag along with therapy and support from friends can bring me joy once again even on my hardest days, where my motivation is nothing, where I hate my makeup, and nothing goes right.

❀ Aging can cause the depression to worsen. When your face and body begin to change and you don't look the same. It can take some time to hopefully change your mindset from ingenue to an aging actress. Find what makeup changes to make and what clothing styles work for your changing body.

❀ Drag is never a cure all. It has shown itself to me even during a performance. To me it is just a outlet to let yourself go into a different world and escape reality. Depression especially for me can manifest at any given time. It's just I have to figure out how to get my head right and in the right state to beat it.

❀ While drag certainly helps as a form of anti-depression it is not the cure. You cannot rely just on drag. You need a great doctor that will work with you to ensure you have the best medicinal cocktail to balance you out. Please don't mask your depression with drag. Drag helps me but it's no guarantee it will help you. Depression does what it wants to whoever whenever it wants.

❀ I was lucky enough to find drag and figure out that it always lifts me up. I cannot always be in drag when depression hits. Drag may not be for everyone. My best advice is that you must figure out where to direct your energy when feeling depressed. I have a collection that I go to catalog or organize and that helps my depression too. It's about redirecting your focus!

❀ Nothing is ever a cure-all for depression, not even medication. You can benefit significantly by using the proper tools, like medication and the outlet of performing. There are times when you get too overwhelmed and nothing can lift your spirits. The most important thing is to go ahead and perform; give it your all even if it takes everything you have to go on stage.

❀ People are foolish to assume that DRAG is a cure-all form of depression. You can have an amazing support system and know that people love and accept you for who you are; there will always be that darkness biding its time in the back of your head to consume your rational thinking when you feel yourself starting to slip.

❀ If I'm not passionate about my performance or it's a last-minute creation then I don't enjoy it I don't get the break from life. I can't get fully into my drag persona and stop being me for a little bit.

❀ It is definitely not a cure-all. There are many ways it can make you more self-conscious. It can also bring a lot of self-deprivation.

❀ I had to actually seek professional help for my depression. When I am too deep in it, I can't perform or plan performing. I have to keep working to get to a place where drag can help pull me further back to myself from the deep despair of depression. I then can utilize all the goodness that comes from doing drag.

❀ I would not say it is a cure all. It can certainly be a portion of your care regime, depending on the severity of your depression. It is healthy, fun, cathartic and it keeps you busy and social. Do not let it also stand in the way of figuring out how else you need to best be taken care of including time off, therapy, medications, professional help, et cetera. One step at a time.

❀ Sometimes it allows me to express what I'm feeling, but that doesn't eliminate the stressor or depression itself. In those times it's a bit of a relief. Like someone helping you carry the weight for a bit, even if its short-lived it still helped me hold on for longer than I thought I could.

❀ I don't feel drag is a cure-all from depression. I feel that if you utilize it properly, no differently than any coping mechanism, it is a tool to be used to help. It can add to depression, for example if you're in a dark place and choose a dark song it can keep you there instead of lifting you out.

❀ It isn't a cure, because there is no cure. We have lost so many beautiful, talented artists, I think due to the belief that if you can reach a certain point, you will be "enough" and find a cure. Drag is an expression, a way of finding a community. Drag is finding your voice and the ears that will listen. It helps, but it isn't a cure.

❀ Nothing on this planet should be a pacifier to your depression. Meditation, coping skills, and the love of your family and friends. Drag does not always save me, as it were. A very good friend taught me this a very long time ago and sometimes it helps. "I choose this day to relive the past, so long as it brings me joy and satisfaction. No longer do I dwell within pain and regret." I believe that regret means so many things for so many people, but for me it means the fight I did not put up against my abusers. Now, years later, regret for me is that I never forgave.

❀ Just because it works for me doesn't mean it'll work for everyone else. Each and every one of us is a unique person with their own interests and passions. Drag works for me but I can't say it's a magic pill for all because I don't know each person.

❀ Well at times someone may have a bad experience in a show or event that breaks the female persona and the flood of thoughts come through. Most times you have to think like an actor or actress, "The show must go on."

❀ It's absolutely not a cure all. It just confirms your existence, your talent and your worth.

❀ Let me start off by saying depression is a disease that is not curable, it is maintained. Some days are good, some days are really bad. Drag helps me get through the rough times, but it does not cure me.

❀ I don't know if there's a "cure-all" for depression. You can do a show and the crowd thinks you were fantastic, but there's a part of you that doesn't agree. You dwell only on what you think, which takes you back to negative thoughts and not the thoughts of someone who enjoyed watching you perform.

❀ There are times depression gets such a grievance that no matter what, I just can't function. In my heart I know it would help me. Serving my community would help me but my mind simply won't let me function.

❀ Entertainers are the celebrities of the gay community. We put ourselves out there to be critiqued and scrutinized, whether it's a pageant or just a show. Not everyone has our best interest and mental well-being in mind. We have gotten hateful comments about everything from weight, makeup, hair, costumes et cetera. If you don't go in with a thick skin or the ability to take criticism then it's easy to get sucked into the negativity and end up feeling worse.

❀ There's no solution to depression. We can find confidence and purpose in our art. Drag gives a vehicle to spread love. Sometimes people do not understand our art and can be hurtful.

❀ Drag helps me get out of own head by using music and the way I dress to express what's going on without really having to say anything. Drag is an outlet for my depression, but not a cure.

❀Drag usually always works for me.

❀ I still get stuck in my head sometimes. Even in the middle of performing, I will drop. I have a really good support system and at least one of them show up to every show. They help ground me and get out of my head so I can enjoy what I'm doing.

❀ Depression is incurable, but can always be countered with uplifting thoughts, memories, scenarios and even the act of playing dress up for photos. The acts of the craft are what you as a person need to focus on. Little negative details like a song you're playing while painting can trigger you down. Be optimistic as much as you can be. Buying alcohol ends up enhancing emotions. Vicious non-ending cycle for some people. Anytime you start Drag you are doing this for you. No one is going on the stage with you.

❀ Drag is an outlet, a distraction, a way to connect with people, and a means to process your emotions. It's not a cure any more than gardening or yoga is a cure. I've also found that it tends to have a greater effect on situational depression - helping you do to deal with what you're currently going through, or what you have been through. If your depression is clinical, it might still help, just not as much. I'm on medication to manage my clinical depression, and the medication is the only thing that consistently helps me manage. When I'm not on my meds, sometimes I'll lose interest in performing. I don't want to be social; I don't want to put the effort in to picking songs and getting ready. When I can't find a song that I feel passionate about, I normally give myself a break from shows until I'm able to get back on my medications again.

🏵 Drag is not a cure all for depression. It can be a crutch if the audience electrified you! Often before hitting the stage, at times my effort is minimal. I've done songs I know because I do them so much. I make it as easy as possible. I'd cancel, if I could, but I rely on the pay.

🏵 Drag is definitely not a cure-all for depression. I still have days where I want to perform but my depression will simply tell me, "No, you're staying in today." When I first started doing drag I did it every week. But that didn't really help my depression when I was starting to stress myself out trying to find looks and music and inspiration.

🏵 Drag works in the moment. The more I do it, the more I don't have to focus on what depresses me. I love to entertain and make people laugh. Making other people happy keeps me happier than I would be without drag.

🏵 While drag can be therapeutic and helpful to work through issues at times it can also be stressful and exhausting. Trying to constantly keep up, create new numbers and stay relevant as a King in a Queen's world burns me out. If I'm already in a dark place, sometimes it's more of a struggle to show up. I know my performances suffer, but the alternative is to stay home and give up which makes me feel even worse like I've failed my fellow performers and fans.

🏵 While drag is an outlet to get rid of some of the emotions I am having. I can say for me it's a band-aid. I find that although it helps, I need to see a therapist too. First and foremost, you have to take care of yourself. Ask for help when you need to get help. I know it's not easy but it does help in the long run.

❀ In reality, nothing is a "cure-all" from depression. Sometimes we just have to ride it out. And many times, in the drag community, things happen. Lots of times the queens you work with misunderstand your depression for sadness, and they can be very judgmental towards people with mental disorders because they don't really understand what's actually happening to a person. This is particularly evident towards people with a social communication disorder, like autism. This misunderstanding can make us spiral lots of times, and question whether we really want to do drag. Even as someone who understands that this can happen in any subculture, it's still hard. But when it comes to depression, things like drag are a tool, a tool we can use to uplift ourselves when we feel depressed. It's not a cure-all. And because of this, sometimes we will still feel depressed. But despite this, drag has still made me happier than I've ever been before. While it's not always a cure-all, it still helps me more often than not.

Chapter Ten, Question Ten
"How do the fans help you with your depression?"

❀ Don't ask your fans to buy you drinks when you are depressed. I promise you; the cocktail will not work. If anything, it will make you more depressed. Use your fans for their appreciation of you. For that moment they are your family. Ask them to continue their love by following you on social media.

❀ Fans can help and hinder my depression. Applause is a fantastic medicine. Something I've had to get used to is a straight woman coming up to me, after a show, and saying "You really did a good job tonight." Like they're surprised. I'd love to answer "Well, darling, I hope so...I've been doing it for over forty years!"

❀ The love and support from them build my confidence and make me feel better about myself. The love they have for entertainers is just amazing and puts me on a high.

❀ The fans are a huge help. I often get messages from them recalling a moment that touched them, a song lyric, a conversation after a show, something shared online. We reach people in many ways, not just when we're on stage. I haven't performed in over three years, but the messages of love, of memories and asking when I'll be on stage again are encouraging. They serve as validation that I got my message of love, positivity and acceptance out. My performances reached people that needed to hear it. If only I could be that person to myself.

❦ The fans are like the wings of the plane... they are the reason I do what I do. They encourage me, especially when I'm not doing well. They are my biggest inspiration, and they make me feel loved and worthy of the stage!

❦ The fans help so much while I'm on stage performing. It makes me feel special when I hear them screaming and cheering for me. All the people telling me how much they love when I perform for them.

❦ My fans help me feel valid. They are the wind beneath my wings and help me remember why I keep fighting the good fight against my depression. So many times, I had fans and friends surround me with big hugs; reminding me why I'm still here. I couldn't ask for anything more.

❦ The fans help me much especially when an entire venue is screaming my songs. I have to say the kids I run into at Pride events probably help me the most. Sure, an adult saying you did great is flattering but to me it means more when a child is looking up at you with wide eyes saying, "I want to be like you." It makes me feel like I'm doing something right.

❦ Oh my God, my fans are wonderful. I have a small fan base of loyal and loving fans. I work at a small venue. I am very open about my life along with my checkered past. So many of them know the real me. Being 62, I have lots of health issues. When I'm in pain they can see it and will help me. I've had fans help me get off the ground. I had another run to the dressing room to get my inhaler. When I'm down they will do their best to lift my spirits. I had a fan actually private message me once because I had been out of the spotlight for a bit too long. He was genuinely worried about my well-being. That is love. I really am one of the luckiest old queens in the world.

❦ My fans help me out tremendously, they are definitely amazing hype men. It definitely makes me think that my arch thought I provide is valid and loved. I'm sure I would still be a shy and anxiety filled as ever but my fans go and support me. Knowing that I have people that will love and support me makes me a little bit happier. My fans and my drag family seem to be my own form of depression medication. Without my fans there would be no stage persona.

❦ The fans I've met over the years really helped me. I remember two women who were best friends coming to the show and having fun afterwards. They came up to me. One of them thanked me and said that her friend husband had passed away. She hadn't smiled for months but she was smiling now. To me that makes it worth it all.

❦ When the world seems stacked against me and I walk out on stage, the thunderous roar and claps makes it all disappear, even if for only a moment.

❦ The fans help me with my depression by cheering me up and treat me like gold. I love when they ask me for advice, makeup tips, take pictures and videos with them, or ask me to send quick video messages to their loved ones celebrating their birthdays, wedding, wedding anniversaries or in some cases when they are at the Hospital waiting for surgery or at the ER. It cheers me up when I cheer others.

❦ When I get into the crowds and the fans want to start hugging. This really gets me into my happy place. My drag exposes my vulnerability which has ways to connect with my fans. My drag serves a purpose to help others and seeing that connection in action really brings joy to my heart. If I can connect with just one of you reading this book, please know you are loved and very much wanted.

❦ The gratitude that I feel for everyone that supports my drag, the adulations, the messages, the applause, and the hugs from fans are why I entertain. I may be the one on stage giving the performance but the audience does not realize that they are giving me so much more!

❦ The fans remind me that what I'm doing is meaningful.

❦ My fans give me a sense of power! They didn't come to hear I'm depressed and not myself or that I'm just not with it today. When I hear them cheer and see them light up when they see me, I feel complete as if I am doing what I should be doing. There is nothing more rewarding then to feel the love and appreciation of your fans!

❦ Fans always boost my energy during and after a show. Some have been able to really pull me up and have become very close friends.

❦ The fans help me with my depression by reminding me of one of the reasons why I wanted to do DRAG in the first place. After a show, I am humbled when people approach me praising me for an amazing performance and asking for my social media handle so that they can follow me. By engaging with me and asking questions about being a DRAG King, I feel loved and supported by the queer community.

❀ My fans help me with my depression by reminding me that I am inspiration to them. Many people will tell me that they are glad I'm breaking social norms of drag and not like a typical drag performer. It honestly brings joy to my heart whenever someone tells me they enjoy watching me perform or just watching me in drag online. Being a drag king is hard at time but I'm glad to have wonderful friends and fans to help lift me up.

❀ Motion creates emotion. Fans get more involved in the show when you make a connection. Fans can make you feel good. They let you know that you did well, what is satisfying, plus having a successful show makes you feel good to perform. In drag specifically, it's like gender validation if your trans and a hell of a compliment if you're not trans. It makes it all worthwhile for me as well as them, when I can have a few drinks and speak with audience members, accept compliments, and thank them for coming. Meeting people feels good. It can be nice. Fans help your depression if you include them. You make a human connection on and off stage. Treat fans well. Meet people after the show. It's good fellowship. If you're not interested in your crowd, they will never be interested in you.

❀ Seeing them smile and forget about their problems while we are on stage, elevates my mood.

❀ The fans help me with depression by being able to see their reactions or interactions with me while performing. As well as when the show is over and they want to come talk to me about the show and get to know me. You begin to realize that there are nice people out there which is what we all need in our lives right now... good people!

❀ The fans' reaction to my song and performance encourages me. They help me forget what's going on in my head. The audience helps change my mind, mood and lifts up my spirit so my depression slowly subsides.

❀ In many ways the fans are the best part of drag by watching them laugh, cry or just enjoy my performance. It fills me with so much love and joy that I can carry it with me when I'm not on stage. They can reach out to me. I can support them and they can support me. It means more than they could ever know, without them drag wouldn't be anything.

❀ The fans are the breath of fresh air when you feel like you're drowning. They're the spark that ignites the fire. Without the ability to feed off the fans good energy performing is lifeless.

❀ The fans play an imperative role in helping me manage my depression as my social support network, especially during the intimate energy exchange between us during my performances. I also really appreciate all of the love, support, and appreciation I receive after each show. It really has a powerful impact on my mood for the rest of the day and sometimes, even the rest of the week. My life experiences are consistently validated by my fans and audience members when I perform acts that speak to them about personal struggles they may relate to. I'm so happy that I'm capable of being vulnerable on the stage to potentially impact someone's quality of life, that fact in itself makes me proud of how far I've come in life. I'm genuinely grateful for all of the humans who have vocally and physically supported me through my drag king journey. I cherish my fan-base and they will always remain a special part of my emotional support system who never fails to make me smile. Lastly, it's such an empowering and exhilarating feeling to experience the loud cheers of the audience during an act where you're sharing such an intimate part of yourself.

❀ Knowing that someone out there not only agrees with and understands my art, but actively enjoys my way of expressing that art, is a huge perspective helper for me. It helps me be objective about my own creativity.

❀ The fans are probably the most lifesaving part of drag. They are the reason I do what I do and they get me to go out there on a stage even if I am severely depressed. Though it really wasn't the same, during COVID my fans cheered me on via video performances and such. Hearing those fans cheer and scream their hearts out, knowing they are here to support all forms of art from drag, burlesque, to dancers; that is what saves my life. I've had fans come up to me after some of my most powerful performance and tell me it'll be okay, that I'll make it through. Some of those fans have become my best friends. Those fans give me a purpose, platform and they truly give me a place to let my emotions out on stage. Without them, I'd be nothing and probably wouldn't be here today.

❀ I always feel weird saying I have 'fans'. Supporters is a better term for me. When I can hear them screaming, when they come up to me after the show to explain how excited they were or how good I did, it's always a great feeling and it hits those neurotransmitters in a positive way. I've had people come up to me just ecstatic that I dressed as their favorite character or even straight men often come up to me to tell me they were surprised with how they found my act sexy! I've had non cis people approach me to say that I inspire their own body confidence. People all around constantly are telling me that they enjoy something 'fresh and new.' This tells me I'm doing it right. When you have a feeling of success, you don't feel like everything is such a huge failure; it inspires me to keep going.

❀ My fans are amazing. The bad thing is, I was always so wrapped up in building walls that I never realized I had fans. Now, with the help of being able to tell my story, my walls have fallen and I have never felt so much love from so many people. Sometimes, my fans save my life.

❀ There is nothing more validating then when someone comes up and says they saw me at Pride three years ago to tell me it made them feel validated seeing someone like me on the stage, I gave them someone to look up to in life, et cetera. Sometimes just hearing that someone sees my effort can be just what I needed during a particularly exhausting spell of depression. I also just enjoy seeing others smile. If I can do that with one of my numbers, it makes me smile too.

❀ Seeing their excitement and the compliments lets you know you are loved and accepted. Th fans allow part of your life to get reassurance that everything is great and wonderful.

❀ I have an amazing fan base; I do stand-up comedy in drag. I discuss hard topics as well as joke about my daily crazy mix-ups and mess-ups. My fans drive my therapy during a show because shows are part of my therapy.

❀ I have the best fans. Male or female, straight, gay, or anything between, young, old, I've performed for damn near everyone in 44 years. I've never been heckled, disrespected, or disappointed.

❀Once on stage and performing my number, the crowd's response and positive reactions help my depression melt away. The support and love you get from an audience for me makes me want to go on to another day.

🌸 I wasn't wanted by my parents or family. My grandmother even told my family members not to tell me I was smart or to cheer me on. She said it would make me work harder. My spirits are lifted and it warms my heart when I do get to perform and the crowd actually cheers for me.

🌸 I'm so thankful for drag fans because they help bring the atmosphere of performing to life! Any time I step into a space that has drag, it is aglow with people who are not only eager to be entertained, but are also equally as eager to spread joy and love to the entertainers there helping pump them up for the show. This also occurs online. The positive comments and messages I receive have made such a huge impact on my drag, lifting me up to new levels of appreciation for drag fans everywhere.

🌸 My fans make me forget about my depression and focus on what I love to do!

🌸 I think I rarely have any fans and the ones that are friends that support my cause probably don't know much besides I get undressed and come out dancing. My ability to pull smiles and give energy is the same. Same as a fan or crowd. I use them to get energy and support. I know I'm not the biggest loser, nor the weirdest amazing star, but my depression isn't thought of when I'm headed to stage. On social media I get tagged in post or memories of prideful events. It just boosts me to come back to give them what they give me: life and courage. Though I still can't get rid of depression. PTSD from earlier years of life will remain. If you're a fan of mine, thank you, besos (kisses).

🌸 The fans pay attention to us, much more than we often realize. Many times, they notice when there's a subtle change in our performance, song choice or behavior off-stage. There have been a few times when a fan has reached out to me to say they noticed such a change, and let me know that they were there for me if I wanted to talk. Whether or not I felt like opening up to them at the time... it meant the world to me to feel seen, and to have the reassurance that they care about me as a person, and not just as an entertainer.

🌸 The love and support I receive when I am in drag, validates my art. This is a huge weapon in my daily battle against depression.

🌸 The fans are amazing in our region. Their smiles and cheering on when performing as a hostess, DJ or a simple number. The fans are stellar and fabulous. Before the event; life shows its true color, a void that cannot be escaped. When I enter the dimly ambient room with smiles a blaze, the mood changes in that state to a state of bliss and happiness. the fans came to see me and the event. The sadness goes away for just a few hours.

❀ The best part of doing drag is the fans. I was in a dark place last month and I had my very first Pride gig ever! A number of fans came up and told me that I inspired them, because I was the only king! I represented the drag kings and the trans performers of my area by going out of town to the gig. Having those people come up to me and tell me they want to start performing was honestly the thing that saved me from myself.

❀ Without the fans there's no need to perform. The fans bring the shows to life. Giving the fans what they like makes me forget about my depression in that moment. It's a time to bask in the ambiance of the stage!

❀ When I see a fan able to relax and let go of their problems for a moment, makes me feel like I have a propose. It lifts my mood exponentially.

❀ The fans put a spark in my soul, a pep in my step. Drag is an outlet for my depression, so when I see and hear that other people were touched by my act, I realize I am not alone. Often my acts reflect my deepest feelings... fear, joy, depression, pain, or even sadness. I see I am not the only one who feels this way when I see the crowd react and feel the same kind of emotion. I know I am ok. Hearing how someone was personally touched by something I did after a show re-enforces this feeling of peace; it eases my brain to know we are not fighting in this crazy world alone.

❀ The fans are what helps me stay out of depression. To see their smiles and words of praise help me to stay happy. I love when people say, "What you did with your energy makes me feel exhilarating!"

❀ The fans are my favorite part! When I'm having a rough patch, feeling like I'm failing as a performer and ready to quit, having fans come up to me and tell me how I've inspired them or how a number has impacted them reminds me why I do drag. It gives the strength to at least hang on until the next show.

❀ I guess I don't really consider them fans, but my community members. They help me by sharing their experiences and connections they made to the performances. These tend to lead to amazing talks and interactions that feed my soul and hopefully theirs as well. This helps with the depression management so much!

❀ I would say that fans help me to a point but they can also do the opposite. When it comes to fans, I always tell them that perception is key and I respond accordingly. Most of the time the love and admiration I get is positive and often helps me. There are also some that will just come for me and it is not helpful at all.

❀ Fans are the product of drag performances. When you perform, the end result is the joy of others. Being able to see that I've helped entertain, educate, inspire, and/or provoke thought in others is the main reason I am happy from my drag. I'm not a celebrity by any means, but I now know why celebrities are always thanking their fans. It really is a genuine gratitude for every single individual out there. We wouldn't have art if we didn't have fans.

❀ Fans always help build you up and they know when your down and are always there to listen.

Ten Black Books of DRAG411.com Are now Twelve books!

Book 1 DRAG411's
"DRAG Bully, A Survivor's Guide"

The Largest Bullying Project in LGBT History for Struggling Entertainers. Advice from over a hundred male, female, and androgynous impersonators around the world to help entertainers struggling with their family, peers, relationships, neighbors, regular jobs, venues, and successfully overcoming self-doubt. Best Selling author Todd Kachinski Kottmeier created DRAG411 to document the lives of male, female, and androgynous impersonator years ago. It is now the largest organization for impersonators on earth with over 7,000 entertainers in 32 countries. DRAG411 also operates The International Original, Official DRAG Memorial with almost two thousand names (2022). This is his 25th book, 20th World Record, and 10th book on this subject. Thousands of invitations to contribute were send out. This book contains the best of their responses, in their own words, to you.

Book 2 DRAG411's
"Original, Official DRAG Handbook"

Over 155 female impersonators (and 1 male impersonator) from around the world share over a thousand insightful comments in the first handbook created of this artform.

Commentary shared with Todd Kachinski Kottmeier included the following contributors of The Original, DRAG Handbook to include Ada Buffet, Adora , Adrian Leigh, Afeelya Bunz, Alisa Summers, Alanna Divine, Alexis De La Mer, Alexis Mateo, Alex Serpa, Allure, Amanda Bone, Amanda Love, Amy DeMilo, Anastaia Fallon, Astasnaia Rexia, Angel gLamar, Angela Dodd, Anita Cox, April Fresh, Ashleigh Cooley, Aurora Sexton, Babette Schwartz, Bailey St. James, Barbra Herr, Barbra Seville, Beverly LaSalle, BJ Stephens, Blair Michaels, Brandon M. Caten, Brianna Lee, Brittany Moore, Brookyln Bisette, Bukkake Blaque London St. James, Cartier Paris, Cathy Craig, Champagne T. Bordeaux, Cherry Darling, Christina Paris, CoCo LaBelle, CoCo Montrese, CoCo St. James, Conundrum, Crystal Belle, Daniel Murphy, Danika Fierce, Daphne Ferraro, Dasha Nicole, Dee Gregory, Deva DaVyne, Diamond Dunhill, Diedra Windsor Walker, Dmentia Divinyl/Eva LaDeva, Echo Dazz, Esme Russell, Estelle Rivers, Eunyce Raye, Felica Fox, Felina Cashmere, Geraldine Queen Cabaret, Ginger Minj, Glitz Glam, Gilda Golden, Horchata, Ima Twat, Ineeda Twat, Jade Daniels, Jade Jolie, Jade Shanell, Jade Sotomayo, Jaeda Fuentes, Jami Micheals, Jay Santana, Jeffrey Powell, Jenna Chambers Tisdale, Jessica Jade, Jocelyn Summers, Jodie Holliday, Joey Brooks, Joshua

Myers, J.P. Patrick, Juwanna Jackson, Kamden Wells, Katrina Starr, Kenny Braverman, Khrystal Leight, Kier Sarkesian, Kiki LaFlare Santangilo, Kitty D'Meaner, Kori Stevens, Krystal Amore Adonis, Lacey Lynn Taylors, Lady Clover Honey, Lady Sabrina, Lady TaJma Hall, Lakeisha Pryce, LeeAnna Love, Leigh Shannon, Lisa Carr, Lola Honey, Madisyn De La Mer, Makayla Rose Devine, Maxine Padlock (Maxi Pad), Melissa Morgan, Melody Mayheim, Michael Wilson, Mike Astermon-Glidden, Mis Sadistic, Miss Conception, Miss Gigi, Mr. Kenneth Blake, Misty Eyez, Monique Michaels, Myah Monroe, Mystique Summers, Nairobi V. D'Viante, Naomi D-Lish, Naomi Wynters, Nicole Paige Brooks, Nikki Dynamite, Nova Starr, Ororo, Patrica Grand, Patricia Knight, Patrica Mason, Pandora DeStrange, Penelope Reigns, Polly FunkChanel, Phiore Star Liemont, Purrzsa Kyttyn, Pussy LeHoot, Raquel Payne, Rhyana Vorhman, Rickie Lee, Rusti Fawcett, Scarlett Fever, Selina Kyle, Shae Shae LaReese, Shealita Babay, Shugah Caine, Stephanie Roberts, Stephanie Stuart, Stormy Vain, Summer Breeze, Sybil Storm, Tabatha Lovall, Tatum Michelle, Teri Courtney, Tiffani Middlesexx, Timm McBride, Toni Davyne, TotiYanah Diamond,Trixie LaRue, Trixie Pleasures, Vegas Platinum, Venus D Lite, Vivika D'Angelo, Wendel Duppert and Wendy G. Kennedy.

Book 3:   DRAG411's
"Crown Me! Winning Pageants"

Hundreds of invitations sent to the titleholders, pageant promoters, judges, and talent show hosts to share their insight on not only winning pageants and contests but also owning the stage every time they perform. Their topics included auxiliary steps to success needed for song selection, dancing, movement onstage, props, backup dancers, creating your own edge, personal interviews, steps to success for winning the talent category every time you step onstage, onstage questions, eveningwear, and creative costuming. They discussed in their own unedited words, wardrobe changes, makeup, hair, shoes, when is the time to compete, qualities needed for a judge, and the top misconceptions of contestants competing in the pageantry systems.

Commentary shared with Todd Kachinski Kottmeier included the following contributors of Crown Me! to include AJ Menendez, Amy DeMilo, Anastacia Dupree, Anson Reign, Bob Taylor, Breonna Tenae, Brittany T Moore, Coco Montrese, Dana Douglas, Darryl Kent, Denise Russell, Dey Jzah Opulent, Freddy Prinze Charming, Gage Gatlyn, Jay Santana , Jayden Knight, Jennifer Foxx, Joey Jay, Kori Stevens, Mis Sadistic, Mykul Jay Valentine, Natasha Richards, Rico Taylor, Sam Hare, Stephanie Stuart, Taina T. Norell, Tiffani Middlesexx, Tori Taylor, Ty Nolan, Vinnie Marconi, and Vivika D'Angelo.

Book 4:   DRAG411's
"DRAG King Guide"

Over 155 male impersonators around the world share over a thousand insightful comments in forty-one chapters.

Commentary shared with Todd Kachinski Kottmeier included the following contributors of The Official DRAG King and Male Impersonators Guide to include Aaron Phoenix, Abs Hart, Adam All, Adam DoEve, AJ Menendez, Alec Allnight, Alexander Cameron, Alik Muf, Andrew Citino, Anjie Swidergal, Anson Reign, Ashton The Adorable Lover, Atown, Ayden Layne, B J Armani, B J Bottoms, Bailey Saint James, Ben Doverr, Ben Eaten, Bootzy Edwards Collynz, Brandon KC Young-Taylor-Taylor, Bruno Diaz, Cage Masters, Campbell Reid Andrews, Chance Wise, Chandler J Hart, Chasin Love, Cherry Tyler Manhattan, Chris Mandingo, Clark Kunt, Clint Torres, Cody Wellch Klondyke, Colin Grey, Corey James Caster, Coti Blayne, Crash Bandikok, Dakota Rain, Dante Diamond, Davion Summers, DeVery Bess, Devin G. Dame, Devon Ayers, Dionysus W Khaos, Diseal Tanks Roberts, D-Luv Saviyon, Dominic Demornay, Dominic Von Strap, D-Rex, Dylan Kane, E. M. Shaun, Eddie C. Broadway, Emilio, Erick LaRue, Flex Jonez, Freddy Prinze Charming, Gabe King, Gage Gatlyn, George De Micheal, Greyson Bolt, Gunner Gatlyn, Gus Magendor, Hawk Stuart, Harry Pi, Holden Michael, Howie Feltersnatch, Hurricane Savage, J Breezy St James, Jack E. Dickinson, Jack King, Jake Van Camp, Jamel Knight, Jenson C. Dean, Johnnie Blackheart, Jonah Godfather of DRAG, Jordan Allen, Jordan Reighn, Joshua K. Mann, Joshua Micheals, Juan Kerr, Julius M. SeizeHer, Jude Lawless, Justin Cider, Justin Luvan, Justin Sider, K'ne Cole, Kameo Dupree, Kenneth J. Squires, King Dante, King Ramsey, Jack Inman, Kody Sky, Koomah, Kristian Kyler, Kruz Mhee, Linda Hermann-Chasin, Luke Ateraz, Lyle Love-It, Macximus, Marcus Mayhem, Marty Brown, Master Cameron Eric Leon, Max Hardswell, MaXx Decco, Michael Christian, Mike Oxready, Miles Long, Mr-Charlie Smith, Nanette D'angelo Sylvan, Nolan Neptune, Orion Blaze Browne, Owlejandro Monroe, Papa Cherry, Papi Chulo, Papi Chulo Doll, Persian Prince, Phantom, Pierce Gabriel, Rasta Boi Punany, Rico M Taylor, Rock McGroyn, Rocky Valentino, Rogue DRAG King, Romeo Sanchez, Rychard "Alpha" Le'Sabre, Ryder Knightly, Ryder Long, Sam Masterson, Sammy Silver, Santana Romero, Scorpio, Shane Rebel Caine, Shook ByNature, Silk Steele Prince, SirMandingo Thatis, Smitty O'Toole, Soco Dupree, Spacee Kadett, Starr Masters, Stefan LeDude, Stefon Royce Iman, Stefon SanDiego, Stormm, Teddy Michael, Thug Passion, Travis Luvermore, Travis Hard, Trey C. Michaels, Trigger Montgomery, Tyler Manhattan, Viciouse Slick, Vinnie Marconi, Welland Dowd, William Vanity Matrix, Wulf Von Monroe, Xander Havoc, and Xavier Bottoms.

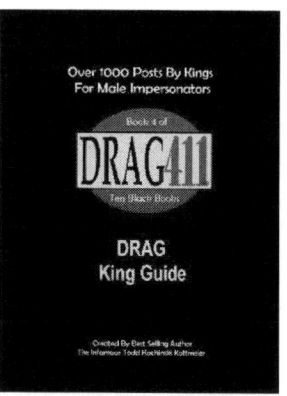

Book 5: DRAG411's
"DRAG Stories"

Funny stories shared with Todd Kachinski Kottmeier including the following contributors of DRAG Stories to include Chance Wise, Anson Reign, Tiffani Middlesexx, Rico Taylor, Todd Kachinski Kottmeier, Bob Taylor, Stefon Royce Iman, Candi Samples, Alexis Mateo, Naomi Wynters, Dmentia Divinyl, Bruce Lacie, Kennedy Wendy, Chastity Rose, Miss GiGi, Angel gLamar, Patricia Grand, Shook ByNature, Lady Guy, Eunyce Raye, Charley Marie Coutora, Jezzie Bell, Lamar Kellam, Jayden St. James, Rachelle Ann Summers, Champagne T Bordeaux, Gilda Golden, Daisha Monet, Vivika D'Angelo, Rachel Boheme, Esme Rodriguez, and MaNu Da Original.

Book 6: DRAG411's
"DRAG Mother, DRAG Father" Honoring Mentors

Performers look to DRAG mothers, DRAG fathers, friends, and fans for insight, compassion, and guidance as mentors. This book honors those special people. Over 140 entertainers contributed wisdom and words for this historical book, making it the largest project of its nature in GLBTQ history and the first published book on male and female mentors.

Commentary shared with Todd Kachinski Kottmeier included the following contributors of DRAG Parents to include AJ Menendez, Vinnie Marconi, Mis Sadistic, Todd Kachinski Kottmeier, Bob Taylor, Taina Norell, Andrew Stratton, Horchata Horchata, VIKKI SHOKK, Gianna Love, Trinity Taylor, Domunique Jazmin Vizcaya, Brittany Moore, PurrZsa Kyttyn, Jake Lickus, Shelita Taylor, Adriana Manchez, MiMi Welch, China Taylor, Armondis Bone't, Monique Trudeau, Simeon Codfish, Diamond Dupree, Stefon Royce Iman, Jayden Stjames, Demonica da Bomb, Colin Grey, Christopher Todd Guy, Celyndra Lashay Clyne, Candice St. James, Justin Barnes Williams, Ivanna Dooche, London Taylor Douglas, Christina Alexandria Victoria Regina Lowe, Bianca DeMonet, Critiqa Mann, Jazmen Andrews, AJ Allen, TotiYanah Diamond, D' Marco Knight, Chip Matthews, Mirage Montrese, India Starr Simms, Jade S Stratton, Emerald Divine, Elysse Giovanni, Vanity Halston, Kristofer Reynolds, Akasha Uravitch, Adriana Fuentes, Erykah Mirage, Felicity Ferraro, Joey Payge, Rhiannon Todd, Vicious Slick, Amirage Saling, Tori Sass, Chy'enne Valentino, and Robbi Lynn.

Book 7: DRAG411's
"Spotlight Today"

It was the World's Largest Paperback Magazine for Impersonators and Fans when it premiered with over 175 pages. DRAG411 no longer prints Spotlight Today Magazine, but here is the re-release of the groundbreaking first edition. Complete articles by Vinnie Marconi, Denise Russell, Tiffani T. Middlesexx, Kristofer Reynolds, Magenta Alexandria Dupree, Butch Daddy, Vivikah Kayson-Raye, Makanoe, Amanda Lay, Thomas DeVoyd, Kevin B. Reed, Glenn Storm, and over 150 impersonators from around the world.

Book 8: DRAG411's
"DRAG Queen Guide"

Almost two hundred female impersonators around the world share over a thousand insightful comments in forty-one chapters.

Almost two hundred female impersonators around the world share over a thousand insightful comments in forty-one chapters. Commentary shared with Todd Kachinski Kottmeier included the following contributors: Alana Summers, Alexis Marie Von Furstenburg, Alize', Aloe Vera, Alysin Wonderland, Amanda Bone DeMornay, Amanda Lay, Amanda Roberts, Amy DeMilo, Anastasia Fallon, Angie Ovahness, Anita Mandinite, Appolonia Cruz, Ashlyn Tyler, Aurora Tr'Nele Michelle, Azia Sparks, Barbie Dayne, Barbra Herr, Beverly LaSalle, Bianca DeMonet, Bianca Lynn Breeze, Blair Michaels, Boxxa Vine, Brandi Amara Skyy, Britney Towers, Brittany T Moore, Brooke Lynn Bradshaw, Candi Samples, Candi Stratton, Candy Sugar, Cathy Craig, Catia Lee Love, CeCe Georgia , Cee-Cee LaRouge-Avalon, Celeste Starr, Chad Michaels, Chevon Davis, Cheyenne Desoto Mykels, Chi Chi Lalique, Christina Collins, Chrystal Conners, Claudia B Eautiful, Coca Mesa, Coco St James, Damiana LaRoux, Dana Scrumptious, ⊛Danyel Vasquez, Dee Gregory, Delores T. Van-Cartier, Demonica DaBaum, Denise Russell, Diamond Dunhill, Diva Lilo, Diva Savage, Dove, EdriAna Treviño, Elle Emenopé, Elysse Giovanni, Erica James, Esmé Rodríguez, Estella Sweet, Eunyce Raye, Eva Nichole Distruction, Faleasha Savage, Felicia Minor, Felicity Frockaccino, Gigi Masters, Ginger Alley, Ginger Gigi Diamond, Ginger Kaye Belmont, Glitz Glam, Grecia Montes D' Occa, Heather Daniels, Hennessy Heart, Hershae Chocolatae, Holy McGrail, Hope B Childs, Horchata, India Brooks, India Ferrah, Ivy Profen, Izzy Adahl, Jaclyn St James, Jade Iroq, Jade Sotomayor, Jade Taylor Stratton, Jamie-Ree Swan, Jennifer Warner, Jessica Brooks, Jexa Ren'ae Van de Kamp, Joey Brooks, Jonny Pride, Kamden T. Rage, Kamelle Toe, Karma Jayde Addams, Kelly Turner, Kira Stone-St James, Kirby Kolby, Kita Rose, Krysta Radiance, Lacie Bruce, Lady Jasmine Michaels, Lady Pearl, Lady Sabrina, LaTonga Manchez, Latrice Royale, Leona Barr, Lexi Alexander, Lilo Monroe, Lindsay Carlton, Lucinda Holliday, Lunara Sky, Lupita Chiquita Michaels Alexander, Madam Diva Divine, Mahog Anny, Makayla Michelle Davis Diamond, Mama Savannah Georgia, Mariah Cherry, Maxine Padlock, Melody Mayheim, Menaje E'toi, Mercede Andrews, Mi$hal, Mia Fierce, Michelle Leigh Sterling, Miss Diva Savage, Miss GiGi, Misty Eyez, Mitze Peterbilt, Monica Mystique, Montrese Lamar Hollar, Morgana DeRaven, Mr. Kenneth Blake, Muffy Vanbeaverhousen, Natasha Richards, Nathan Loveland, Nicole Paige Brooks, Nikki Garcia, Nostalgia Todd Ronin, Olivia St James, Paige Sinclair, Pandora DeCeption, Pheobe James, Reia'Cheille Lucious, Rhonda Sheer, Robyn Demornay, Robyn Graves, Rose Murphy, Ruby Diamond NY, Ruby Holiday, Ryan Royale, Rychard "Alpha" Le'Sabre, Rye Seronie, Sable Monay, Sabrina Kayson-Raye, Samantha St Clair, Sanaa Raelynn, Sapphire T. Mylan, Sasha Phillips, Savannah Rivers, Savannah Stevens, Selina Kyle, Sha'day Halston-St James, ShaeShae LaReese, Shamya Banx, Shana Nicole, Shaunna Rai, Sierra Foxx White, Sierra Santana, Sonja Jae Savage, Stella D'oro, Strawberry Whip, Sugarpill, Tanna Blake, Taquella Roze, Tasha Carter, Tawdri Hipburn, Taylor Rockland, Tempest DuJour, Tiffani T. Middlesexx, Traci Russell, Trudy Tyler, Vanessa del Rey, Velveeta WhoreMel, Vera Delmar, Vicky Summers, Vita DeVine, Vivian Sorensin, Vivian Von Brokenhymen, Vivika D'Angelo-Steele, Wendy G. Kennedy, Willmuh Dickfit, Wynter Storm, Yasmine Alexander, and ZuZu Bella.

Book 9:DRAG411's (Two Comedy Scripts)
"Best Said Dead" and **"Following Wynter"**

Best Said Dead examines in funny conversations those brief minutes after a person dies. Many religions and beliefs define different paths for each of us. Rarely do we discuss those precious moments between death and the final destination. This comedy opens the possibilities that for a moment, a person vanishes into the memories in their mind. Any part can be male, female, or ambiguous.

Following Wynter is a hilarious comedy play. Ethan discovers his newlywed husband is the flamboyant DRAG Queen Wynter Storm in this whimsical farce with an important message of believing in yourself and your friends. . . even if your friend is Serena Silver. Any part can be male, female, or ambiguous.

Book 10: DRAG411's
"DRAG World"
The contributing writers of DRAG411's "Spotlight Magazine," the World's Largest Paperback Magazine for Impersonators and Fans when it premiered in 2012 with over 175 pages, created this companion book. DRAG411 no longer prints Spotlight Today Magazine, but above you will find Book 7 is the re-release of the groundbreaking first edition. Complete chapters on DRAG Marketing by DRAG411.

Complimentary articles on Confidence, Duct Tape, Music Selection, Living Divinely, authentic stage presence, Pageants, having fun performing, jewelry, legislative information from the United States and around the world, the Old School performers, Virgin stage performers, and payday from contributing writers including Denise Russell, Jay Santana, Chance Wise, Vivikah Kayson-Raye, AJ Menedez, Glenn Storm, Freddy Prinze Charming, Gage Gatlyn, Kevin B. Reed, and over 100 impersonators from around the world!

Book 11: DRAG411's
"The DRAG Book"
Ten books, that was supposed to be the challenge when the publisher was diagnosed with onset dementia, but the Infamous Todd Kachinski Kottmeier knew he could challenge himself to document a few more DRAG stories and lessons. This is hundreds and hundreds of performers sharing their advice to performers across the world through over fifty questions.

Commentary shared with Todd Kachinski Kottmeier included the following contributors A'ryiah Monè Diamond, Aaliyah Tealheart, Abs Hart, ADHD, Adriana Manchez, Adriana Mariee Kardashh, Aero Dean, Afro❀Deity, Alexander Moonwalker Knightly Jackson, Alexander Stryke, Alexandre Valentino Skye, Alexandro Rox, Alexis De La Mer, Alexis Milan, Alexis von Furstenberg, Alexye'us Paris, Allie Waye, Amadeus X Machina, Amanda Bone DeMornay, Amanda D Rhod, Amanda Playwith, Ambrosia S Thorne, Amy DeMilo, Andrea Forwards Anhedonia Delight, Anitta Schwanz, Aniya Stars, AnnaStaysha, Anne Drogyny, Ariana Autumn, Ariana Love, Astara Love, Auda Beaux Di, Aura Glitz, Aurora F. Sterling, Aurora LeKohl, Aurora Nicole, Aurora Risay, Aurora Veil, Autumn Holiday, Avery Rose Norwood, Azaria Kimberly Vallium, Barbie Dayne, Barbie Dicks, Barbra Herr, Bearonce Bear, Beau D. Vyne Bianca Blak, Bianca L'Amour Billy Jean, BinKyee Bellflower, BJ Bottoms, Blair Which, Blu Shady, Blyss Carrington, Bonni Blake, Bran Ray Lavo, Brandon KC Young-Taylor, Brandon Race, Brendan Bravado, Brock Harder, Bronzie De'Marco Bubonic Rose, Buttwiser, Cake Moss, Candie Hearts, Candy Buttons, Carly Uninemclite, Carmen Love, Carnelian Clinique Carnita Asada, Carter Bachmann, Casanova, Cass Marie Domino, Catastrophē Nicole Knight, Cathy Craig, CC, Charlie Mornett von Trash, Chase Sky, Cher Michaels, Cheri Bomb LeKohl, Cherilyn Matthews, Chevelle Chardonnay, Chiffon Dior, Christian Mingle, Christina Collins, Christopher Allure, Christopher Peterson, Clara Tea, Colin Grey, Crystal Blu, CupCake, Daisy May, Dani Panic, Danilo De la Torre, ❀Danyel Vasquez, Daphnie Moonwalker Rains, Deandra Dee Paige, Dee Dee Van Carter, DeeDee Marie Holliday, Deja Van Cartier, Delores T. Van-Cartier, Demona Frost, Denise Russell, Derek Skye Villaverde, Desiree DeMornay Destinē Brookes, Destiny B, Childs, Diego Wolf, Diva Kingsley, Diva Lilo, Diva Savage, Dizzy Grant Diamandis, D-Luv Saviyon, Dolly Bee Wellington, Donny Mirassou, Dovey Diabolique, Dr. Rasta Boi Punany, Dre Seymour-Mykals, Dunkin Dame, Dymond Onasis, Eazy Love Eddie Edwards, Edna D Mascará, Eileen Taylor Elle Taylor, Elyce Michaels, Erica St, Michaels, Erotica Romance, Estella Sweet, Eunice Alexander, Eva Dystruction, Evian Waters, Evona Valentino James, Felicia Minor, Felicity Foxhaven, Fiera Ice, Flame E Morning-Star DeMornay, Frank Lee, Frothy La Frou Frou, Galaxÿ, GatorDunn, Genevee Ramona Love, Gina D'licious, Ginger Beer, Gorgina George, Gyp'C Royal, Harpy Daniels, Hazel Derèon, Helena Handbasket Helix Rider, Henni C, Hershae Chocolatae, Holly Louya, Hunta Downe, Hunter Downs Morgan, Ian Syder-Blake, Idina Rimes, Imani Valentino, Iris Fay Moonwalker, irishimo, Ivana B, Real, Ivy League, Jade DeVere, JaJa Ohmai Whoremoans, James Cass, Jamie Cole, Jamie Monroe, Jasmine Skyy, Jason Beauregard, JC Rios, Jenna Starr, Jennifer Foxx, Jennifer Lynn, Jessica Deveraux, Jessica L'Whor, Jessica Patterson, Joanna James, Jodie Santana, Joey Brooks, Joey Gallagher, Josie Purée, Justice Twist, Justin Deeper-Love, Justyn Caze, Juuls, Kade Jackwell, Kahtya Tehnsion, KaiKai Bee Michaels, Kaleigha Diamond, Kamden T. Rage, Kandi Dishe, Kara Belle, Kathryn Nevets, Kay Fierce, KayKay Lavelle Kelasia Karmikal, KHAOS, Ki'Arra Infiniti-Ross, KiKi Mamah, King Blaze Khrystian, King Chris Dingo, King Crimson, King Perka $exxx , Kitt Raven, Kitty Litter Konstance Panic, Kruz Mhee, Krystal Cain, Krystal Cassadine, Krystal Naomi, Kyla G'Diva Rogue, Lacie Bruce, Lady Cynthia, Lady Inferno Diamond, Lady Sabrina, Lady Seduca, Ladycat De'Ore, Lamia - The Cursed Queen, LeKross DeAire Menendez, Leota Tombs, Lethia Dose, Liam Axel, Liquor Mini, Logan Rider, London Divine Sinclaire, Lori Divine, Luci Furr-Matrix, Lucy Paradisco LUST, M.C. Rawr, Madam D, Madame

Fellatia Monroe, Makayla Rose Devine, MaKayla Styles, Martini, Matt Cockrin, Maxum Delray, Melissa Mason, Melody Lush, Mia Inez Adams, Michael Kane, Miles N. Sider Austin Mischa Michaels Miss Conception, Miss Domeaner MorningStar, Miss Piss, Molly Mormen, Momma Ashley Rose, Momma, Mona Lotz, Monique Michaels-Alexander, Morgan Davis, Morgana de Luxe, Mr. Killin Ya Softly, Muffy Rosenberg, Muni Tox, Mystique Summers, Naomi DeMornay, Natalie L. Carter, Nick D'Cuple, Nicole DuBois, Nikki Ontolodge Monet, Nikki Saxx, Nikki Silva, Nikoli Popov, Norma Llyaman, Oliver Steerpike, Ophelia Bottoms, Ophelia Handful, Osiris Romanov, Paisley Parque, Pandora DeStrange, Parris B. Cbello, Patrice Knight, Patricia Del Rosario, Patricia Mason, Patty Cakes, Paula Jenkins, PheYonce Montrese Pierce Gabriel, Piranha Del Rey Porsha DeMarco Douglas, Preston Steamed, Prince Kodhi Black Khrystian, Prince Silk St, James, Prinze Valentino, PurrZsa Kyttyn Azrael, Queen Issa Fella, Ramona Mirage, Ravion Starr Alexandria St James, Reba MacIntosh, Rebel Rose, Red Scare, Redd FaFilth, Renita Valdez, Richard La Petite, Rico Taylor, Robyn Hearts, Rockell Blu, Romeo Casanova, Romonica DiGregory, Rouge Fatale, Royale Payne, Ruby James Knight, Sally West, Salma Love Taylor, Sanaa Raelynn, Saniya Chanel Iman, Santana Romero, Sapphire Mylan, Sasha Turrelle, Sassy Sascha, Saylor Alexander Vontrell, Sean Wolff, Senpai, Serra Tonan Savage, ShaeShae LaReese, Shane West, ☙Shasta McNastie, Shaunna Rai, Shelita Taylor, Shire Paige, Sho Sho Zahav, Sina Kakes, Sir Labia Sister Alphena Omega, Skarlet Overkill, Soluna LaVie-Mason Spring Summers, St. Reign, Staci Sings, Starr Shine, Stephanie Stuart, Sue Purr Nova, Suga Avery Bottoms, Sugar Vermonte, Sunny Banks Zane Paige, Sylas Crow, Talia Secret, Tank TopOff, Tara Nicole Brooks, Tara Shay Montgomery, Taylor Dame, Teri Lovo, Teri Taylor, Tia Douglas, Tierra Stone, Tina Louise, Tommy Boy, Tova Ura Vitch, Traynbow, Treasure Rose, Trixie Deflair, Trixy Valentine, Tucker Bleu, Tucker Downtown, Tuesdae Knyte, Twila Starr, Valentino Rose, Valerie Rockwell, Vera DelMar, Veranda L'Ni, Veronica Fox, Veronica Sledge, Versage, Vicki Vincent, Victoira Styles, Victoria Michaels, Victoria Obvious Queen, VIKKI SHOKK, Vinnie Marconi, Vintage Blue, Vivian Von Brokenhymen, Vivika D'Angelo Steele, VonScene, Vyki Z LaRoxx, Wanda Wheeler, Wendy G. Kennedy, Willy Hardt, Xander Morgan Valentine, Xavier Bottoms, Xiomarie LaBeija, Zoe Bitters, and Zoey Zegai.

Alexander Moonwalker Jackson, Alexis von Furstenberg, Amanda Bone DeMornay, Amber Rains, Andrew Martinez, Angel Sexton, Angus McVag, Aniya Stars, Anna Flactic-Shoqqqq, Anna Mae Ceres, Apollo King, Atlas Midos, Aurora F. Sterling, Averi Aycock, Azunique Steely, Bender Nova, Billie King, Brandon Race, Braxton Hicks, Brendan Bravado, Bryce Culver, Bubonic Rose, Buttwiser, Cameron Ticey, Candi Lachey, Canya Bendher, Carter Bachmann, Cathy Craig, Chaella Montgomery-Kohl, Charlemagne Chateau, Chase Hart, Christian Gaye, Christina Collins, Cliff Hanger, Coca J Mesa, Dante Gabbana, Dante Inferno, Danyel Vasquez, DeeDee Bustier, DeeDee Marié J Holliday, Demona Frost, Denise Russell, Dev'on Ess Lee, Diego Wolf, Dik Carrier, Diva Lilo, Donny Mirassou, Dr. Rasta Boi Punany, Dylan B. Dickherson White, Essence Peruu, Evan Bangor, Fallon Vain, Fancy Kakes, Fanny DeVito, Fay-Talie Raynbow DeMornay, Fluxx Wyldly, Freddy Prinze Charming, Frieda Poussáy, Gloria Diamond, Grandma Pearl, Hayden Lee Sunshine, Heather Marie "TaterSalad" Thomas, Hunny Lamp Rotton LaChoy, Idle King, Ima Hoot, Ivy Dripp, Jacquelynn Gillian, James Jackson, Jason Beauregard, Jennifer Foxx, Jessica Emms, Jessica Patterson, Jushtin Butterfly, Justice Twist, Justin Case, Justin Sane, Justin Tyme, Kade Jackwell, Kai, Kale Green, KC StarrZ, Keisha Kye, Kelly Powers, Kenneth J. Squires, Ki'Arra Infiniti-Ross, King Blaze Khrystian, King KJ Mac, King Mykal Khrystian, King Vaughnz Spanic, Kruz Mhee, Lady Cynthia, Lady Laquelle, Ladybug Valentino, Lakeisha Pryce, Lakia Mondale, Levi U.

Wantan Moore, LouAnn Behold, Maya M. Monroe, Michael Monroe, Mischa Michaels, Miss Conception, Miss Domeanor, MissDomeaner MorningStar, Mistress Detta, Mona Del Rose, Mona Lotz, Mondo Millions , Morgan Davis, Mr. Killin Ya Softly, Mrs. PurrZsa Kyttyn Azrael, Mya Chanel Lamour, Neeko Mac, Nick D'Cuple, Nicki Divine, Nik El, Nikki Ontolodge Monet, Nipples LaRue, Oliver Clozoff, Oliver Steerpike , Onyx Reigns, Paisley Parque, Parris B. Cbello, Patrice Knight, Pierce Gabriel, Poppa Pimple, Prinze Valentino, Raquel DeLorean, Rebel Love Diva , Rebel Rose, Renita Valdez, Rockell Blu, Romeo Casanova, Ronnie Belle, Russell Mania, Santana Romero, Sara Hearts, Sassy Black, Savannah Rose Rivers, Scarlett Dailey, Sean Wolff, Selena Gonzales, Serena Hadley, Shae Kain, ShaeShae LaReese, Shane West, Shasta McNastie, Shire Paige, Sïr Vïx, Snowy Marie, Sondra St. James, Special K Culver, STACI, Suga Avery Bottoms, Summer Rayne, Tara Byte, Tasha Dane, Teri Taylor, Tessa Martinez, Tierra Stone, Tina Louise, Tobe Danieles, Tommy Boy, Tonna McKenzie, Travis Hard, Traynbow, Tristan Panucci Dupree, Vanessa Rae Peterson, Vera DelMar, Vicki Vincent, Vinnie Marconi, Warumono, Whiskey Richards, Xavier Bottoms, Xyvien and Zayne "The Dragon" RiAll.

From The Publisher of The Annual Production of

Upcoming Book
DRAG 2.0: The Future of DRAG Releases in 2023

Printed in Great Britain
by Amazon